Promises to Keep

Parents & Confirmation

JOHN-PAUL SHERIDAN

First published 2004 by
Veritas Publications
7/8 Lower Abbey Street
Dublin 1
Ireland
Email publications@veritas.ie
Website www.veritas.ie

ISBN 1 85390 885 1

A catalogue record for this book
is available from the British Library.

Icon on front cover used with permission of the
Russian Ecumenical Centre, Rome.

Extract from 'Stopping by Woods on a Snowy Evening' by Robert
Frost from *The Poetry of Robert Frost*, edited by Edward Connery
Latham and published by Jonathan Cape. Used by permission of the
Estate of Robert Frost and the Random House Group Ltd.

Cover design by Colette Dower
Printed in the Republic of Ireland by Betaprint, Dublin

Veritas books are printed on paper made from the wood pulp of
managed forests. For every tree felled, at least one tree is planted,
thereby renewing natural resources.

The woods are lovely, dark and deep.
But I have promises to keep,
And miles to go before I sleep,
And miles to go before I sleep.

Contents

Introduction 7

Chapter 1 The *Alive*-O Programme 13

Chapter 2 The Holy Spirit 39

Chapter 3 The Sacrament of Confirmation 54

Chapter 4 Other Perspectives on the
Sacrament of Confirmation 70

Prayers for the Year 90

Notes 103

Bibliography 107

 Introduction

A Promise Realised

Every year the Sacrament of Confirmation is celebrated in parishes throughout Ireland. It is a time of grace in the life of a child, their parents and families, and in the life of the parish community to which they belong, however tentative that link is. With the arrival of the new Primary School Catechetical Programme, *Alive-O* to the classes where this sacrament is celebrated, it is as good an opportunity as any to give parents a chance to reflect on what is happening on the day of Confirmation and all that has been happening during the preparation for the Sacrament in schools and sometimes in parishes; preparation that has been carried out by dedicated and wonderful teachers who live out part of their Christian vocation as the mentors and guides of the children. Pedagogy, or the study of education comes from the term *pedagogue*, which refers to the slave who, in Roman times, accompanied children to school. Usually well-educated, they taught the children as they undertook the journey every day. In terms of religious education no term is more fitting for teachers; men and women who walk with the children, guiding them, nurturing and teaching them on the children's journey of faith.

When I was growing up there was only one place that you could buy olive oil and that was in the chemist shop. The oil was really only used for medicinal purposes. Now you can buy all types of olive oil and use it in a huge variety of ways. It is no longer limited to one particular use.

Similarly, in the past we limited how we interpreted the day of Confirmation and we limited what we meant by the Sacrament of Confirmation. We talked about being a 'Soldier of Christ' and being 'filled with the gifts of the Holy Spirit'. To limit how we interpret the sacrament limits the potential for us to understand what Confirmation can really mean for each one of us. This is a great disservice. Confirmation is not a graduation ceremony; it is not a milestone to mark so many years of membership in the church. It should not be given automatically and should not be taken for granted. Confirmation is much more than this. It is so much more, that we haven't even got the language to fully express the power of God at work, not just in the candidates for Confirmation but in the lives and hearts of the entire community.

For parents the day of Confirmation is the culmination of what was begun the day they brought their child to the church to be baptised. On that day they promised to raise their children in the faith that they themselves had been. In one of the final prayers of the Rite of Baptism, the priest prays that as these parents will be the first teachers of their children in the ways of faith, they may also be the best of teachers. On the day of Confirmation that promise comes to fruition. While this work of handing on the

You have asked to have your child baptised. In doing so you are accepting the responsibility of training them in the practice of the faith. It will be your duty to bring them up to keep God's commandments as Christ taught us, by loving God and our neighbour. Do you clearly understand what you are undertaking?

Reception of the Child – *Rite of Baptism*

faith to their children is far from over, the work and witness, the dedication and commitment of parents finds them in their parish church with their family, friends, and possibly the parish community to celebrate an important moment in the lives of all involved.

As happens in some cases, parents have been remiss in handing on the faith, and have rather left this job to the dedicated teachers mentioned earlier. It is one of the regrettable signs of the times that some are unwilling to accept the challenge to educate their children religiously. This can happen for a myriad of reasons and it is not for me or anyone else to make a value judgement on this. We live in a very different Ireland to that of our parents and grandparents – things were far more assured, life was simpler.

Now in this year of Confirmation there is the opportunity to renew the commitment that parents made at the baptism of their children, and become interested in the work being done, the preparation being undertaken, and the possibility and potential for grace in the lives of so many people being realised. To put it in other words I offer an analogy.

Picture the scene, your son or daughter arrives home from school and announces that they have been picked to play for the school team in some major schools league happening this year. There is great enthusiasm and pride and you are delighted for your child. You promise to help them in all the preparation and hard work that will happen over the next few months as the team get ready. You drive them to training sessions and encourage them from the sideline. On the drive home and during countless times at the dinner table you talk strategy and skill, encourage where there is room for improvement and offer suggestions for difficulties they are experiencing. You played yourself in your day and want to offer all the advice and knowledge you learned in the past, and you praise them as their technique improves and their confidence grows. Your child wins the various matches right up along the league and eventually the final looms on the horizon. You offer to buy them new sports gear. The day of the big match arrives and you get all the relatives and friends to attend. The neighbours are there to encourage on the team and your child. The school comes out in force and the local park is full of supporters from all sides. The game begins and your child is playing the best they ever did. You are so proud, especially when they score a few points, and help lead the school team to a resounding victory. The final whistle blows and you are ecstatic. As the celebrations get under way you are approached by the manager of the county team, who congratulates your child on their performance. His parting words are that if they continue to play like that, that he'll be looking for them in a few years time to play for the county. This is the icing on the cake – the possibility of playing for the county. Eventually everything calms down and you head home for a big celebration. In the days following your child takes their new gear, and the medal that they won and puts them into the back of the wardrobe. They never play again. What a tragedy something like that would be. All that training, all that skill, all that potential wasted.

While I'm not equating a sports event in school with the Sacrament of Confirmation, the analogy is not that dissimilar to what often happens after the Sacrament of First Holy Communion and/or the Sacrament of Confirmation in Ireland today. Constantly and often, on visits to schools prior to Confirmation I am struck by the wonderful children that are preparing for the sacrament, and the potential that will hopefully be realised for the future life of the church. Sadly, too often this is unrealised. Confirmation becomes all about the big day and little else after that. It has been often called, rather cynically, the sacrament of exit: you make your Confirmation and then leave the church, your faith, your commitment and everything else so earnestly studied and learned is forgotten or ignored.

This book is offered to parents as an aid to help them engage with the preparation that is being undertaken in school and hopefully in the parish also. Chapter 1 is a general introduction to the *Alive-O* programme, which is now being taught in the 5th and 6th classes. Specific reference is made to the *Alive-O 7* and *Alive-O 8* programmes, explaining the general themes for the years and a brief introduction to the lessons being taught in the 5th and 6th classes. It then makes specific mention of the material being covered in relation to the preparation for the sacrament over the two years of 5th and 6th classes. In Chapter 2, I offer some insight into the Holy Spirit, with specific mention of the Fruits, Gifts, and Symbols of the Holy Spirit. In chapter 3, the concept of Sacrament is explained and the history of the Sacrament of Confirmation is talked about, along with the various elements that make up the celebration of the sacrament. In chapter 4, I suggest some other perspectives on the preparation and celebration of Confirmation regarding some of the theological, sociological and psychological facets of the changing child and emerging adolescent. I have also made passing mention of some of the other aspects usually associated with the preparation and celebration of the sacrament: alcohol and drugs, and the day itself.

The book also includes the prayers that are learnt

in school as part of the *Alive-O* programme, and which are part of the Confirmation preparation.

This book is offered as a guide, as a form of revision, as assistance to parents. It is by no means an exhaustive or comprehensive study on any of the topics mentioned or explored here. I have relied on the considerable wealth of knowledge of others, a bibliography of which can be found at the end.

I wish to thank Maura Hyland of Veritas for asking me to undertake this project and the staff at Veritas for the considerable assistance, most notably Majella Cullinane and Helen Carr. To the writers of the *Alive-O* programme and the members of the Consultation Group who have been a constant source of inspiration over my two years membership of the group, in particular Dr Clare Maloney, Frances O'Connell and Brendan O'Reilly. To Drs Liam Tracey, OSM and Finola Cunnane, SSL, and to Fr Brian Manning for their advice and comments. To my colleagues in St Senan's Parish: Brian and Jason, I thank their endless patience with my attendance at yet another meeting, and thanks also to my colleagues among the National Association of Primary Diocesan Advisors. Finally to Liz, Greg, Conor, Cathy and Tony, my siblings: who might find this useful, either sooner in the case of some, or later in the case of most!

Chapter 1

The *Alive-O* Programme

In 1973 the Conference of Bishops in Ireland decided to update the Primary Religious Education Programme and appointed a team to write a syllabus for the primary schools for the island of Ireland. Teachers welcomed its introduction in 1976, comparing it favourably to the programmes and materials available for other subjects at that time. The programme was innovative and was even adapted for use in English speaking countries throughout the world. It presented the mystery of Christ in all its richness in a gradual way to children as they grew and developed. It drew upon all the sources of God's revelation for its content: Bible, Liturgy, Church Teaching, Christian Witness and the life experience of the children.

One of its major innovations was the recognition of the different but complementary roles of parent/guardian, teacher and priest/parish in the religious education of children. Though the programme set out to help the teacher in the classroom setting, it also recognised that it is

'Beginning school means, for the child, entering a society wider than the family, with the possibility of greater development of intellectual, affective and behavioural capacities.'

GDC 179

those at home who have the primary responsibility in forming the child's faith, and that priests and the parish community also have an important contribution to make in the process. The *Children of God* series was revised in 1983, but even at that time it was seen that a more concise revision needed to take place. In the light of the success of the programme, but conscious of its faults and shortcomings and the fact it has been around for twenty years, it was decided that the programme would be re-presented and that work of re-presentation began in 1993.

In the years since the first introduction of the *Children of God* series, Ireland has changed considerably. In 1999 Martin Kennedy, who writes extensively on religious education in Ireland, was asked to consult teachers, children and priests on their attitudes towards the *Children of God* series. He reported his findings in an article for *The Furrow*.

> *There is good news and bad news in the report. The good news is that both teachers and students are highly positive about the programme – the classroom emerges as a space where the students engage with religion in a way that is delightful for them. The bad news is that the classroom is increasingly the only space where the students so engage with religion. While in theory the religious education of children involves a partnership of home, parish and school the reality appears to be quite different.*[1]

He wrote about the concept of the 'three islands of religious experience' for children: the school, the home and the parish. Children inhabit these three worlds and in terms of an experience of faith, the biggest is that of the school. More and more there is a drifting apart of the three 'islands'. Sometimes the faith expressed in the school bears little or no relation to the faith that is expressed (or not) in the home or in the parish. Any catechetical programme 'worth its salt' must address this issue and provide resources to foster links between these islands.

However, as time goes on many involved in primary religious education see the island of the school getting bigger and bigger, while the island of the home and the island of the parish are shrinking away, almost to the point of extinction. The speed of cultural change in Ireland in the first years of the new millennium has given educators much to contemplate with regards to the effectiveness of religious education in a changing world.

The *General Directory for Catechesis* acknowledges that often the first victims of the spiritual and cultural crisis gripping the world are the young,[2] and suggests that catechesis 'should be proposed in new ways which are open to the sensibilities and problems of this age-group.'[3] A necessary 'adaptation of catechesis for young people is urged, in order to translate into their terms 'the message of Jesus with patience and wisdom and without betrayal'.[4]

The *Primary School Religious Education Programme* (hereafter referred to as the *Alive-O* programme) is one of the ways that the Irish Church seeks to meet the change, and be challenged by it. The aim and explanation of the programme is taken from the general introduction to the teacher's book:

> *As we try and enable the children to grow as people of faith, we hope that they will*

The speed of cultural change in Ireland in the first years of the new millennium has given educators much to contemplate with regards to the effectiveness of religious education in a changing world.

become as articulate in this area as in any other area of the curriculum. We hope that eventually they will be able to give an account of their own faith, to say what they believe and why. This familiarity with the content of faith will be achieved gradually as the children move from class to class, and as their ability to understand difficult language and concepts increases. Faith, however, is not only something to be understood, it is also something to be lived.[4]

The title of the series comes from a quotation from St Irenaeus – 'The glory of God is people fully alive'– and the programme acknowledges as many aspects of children's lives as possible. When referring to a religious education programme, the term catechesis is often used. The term refers to religious education but it takes it a step further. It is also religious formation. It means that when we are learning about faith, our faith is being formed and nurtured. The *General Directory for Catechesis* calls it the 'sublime science of Christ'[6] and states that there are fundamental tasks of catechesis. These tasks are the building blocks of any religious education programme and they are carefully attended to in the *Alive-O* programme. They are: promoting knowledge of the faith; liturgical formation; moral formation; teaching to pray; education for community life; missionary initiation.

Promoting Knowledge of the Faith
In religious education in the past it was all too easy to pick up a Catechism and learn off a series of answers. Well, maybe it wasn't necessarily easy, but this type of approach to knowledge of faith left

people knowing the *what* without necessarily knowing the *why*. In the *Alive-O* programme there is a desire to help children not only advance in their knowledge of faith, but also give them the opportunity to respond to that knowledge in faith. The children learn that faith is a relationship with God, that it is our assent to what God tells us; faith is also a gift from God and our response to that gift; it is both active and communal; faith has a content and it challenges us to work for the kingdom of God.

> *The task of the teacher is to accompany children on their faith journey. Generally speaking this journey will have commenced before any encounter between the teacher and any particular group of children and it will continue long after the encounter. It is a journey of discovery on which the children not only grow in their knowledge of God, but come to know God as someone who loves and cares for them personally.*[7]

Liturgical Formation
In the course of the Primary School, a child will receive the Sacraments of First Holy Communion, Reconciliation and Confirmation. Apart from these, for most children there is a constant exposure to the liturgical life of the Christian community. The programme in Junior and Senior Infants focuses on the four seasons and then from 1st class onwards the programme has many lessons based on the liturgical year: Ash Wednesday and Lent; Easter and Pentecost; the months of October and May for Mary; Advent and Christmas; November and the Commemoration of the Dead. Each year the children are introduced to an Irish saint and by the

end of 6th class they will be familiar with the Seven Sacraments of the Church, will know the various prayers and responses of the Mass, and will have learned the mysteries of the Rosary. It is important that this liturgical formation is done according to their young age and faith, and so it is done over the eight years of primary school. However, and this is essential, liturgical education will fail abysmally if it becomes something that is only done in school. By showing children that going to Mass is not something that you just do in school; that the sacred and spiritual dimension of feasts such as Christmas, Easter, St Patrick's Day and so on are not just the dimension reserved for school, we give the children an opportunity to grow in faith beyond the confines of the school.

Moral Formation

As with liturgical formation, moral formation is taught according to the age, young faith and psychological development of the child. From learning that they are special little individuals (me) in Junior Infants, they move on to learning about having to think of others in Senior Infants (you and me), to learning that there is a wider community in 1st Class (us).

> *Christian Moral Education includes teaching children to love and worship God and to live moral lives as a response to God's love. It involves developing in them an awareness of sin and a sense of penance. It also includes teaching them to follow and imitate Jesus Christ in his love of God and of all people, in his forgiveness of others and in his endurance in suffering.*[8]

The function of moral formation is not to burden the children with a sense of guilt from an early age. The function is to show that they are not the only people in the equation; that they must think of others, that they must share and take turns and must learn to live with one another as best they can. In a time when family sizes are getting smaller, it is often in play-school or in school that children begin to learn socialisation skills for the first time. The point of departure in all this is the abiding, never-ending love of God. This is the image of God that is at the heart of moral formation, and it is this image that the children will learn in the *Alive-O* programme. Again, like liturgical formation, it is impossible to nurture this in the faith life of the child without the help of parents.

Teaching to Pray
It would seem obvious that prayer is the centre of the *Alive-O* programme. It is the opportunity to respond in faith to all that the children are learning in the class and around them.

> *The children's faith in God is fostered through prayer, and they can learn to express this faith in prayer. Teaching children to pray is not the same as teaching definitions of prayer, nor is it as simple as teaching prayer formulas – though this is also important and is accommodated in the programme.*[9]

The children develop an awareness of God's presence in the ordinary events of life. They learn to pray as a response to the things they learn about in school and the experiences they have there. There is a strong sense in the programme of cultivating an atmosphere of prayer, and the use of candles, religious images and music all help the children to

There is a strong
sense in the
programme of
cultivating an
atmosphere of prayer
and the use of
candles, religious
images and music all
help to realise that
prayer time in class is
not the same as every
other part of the day.

realise that prayer time in class is not the same as every other part of the day. They learn the formal prayers such as morning and night prayers, grace before and after meals, (even a grace before and after play); they learn the parts of the Mass and the rosary, and the other prayers of the Catholic tradition; they learn different expressions of prayer: vocal, meditative, contemplative and prayer through movement; and different forms of prayer: prayers of petition, of thanksgiving, of praise, of sorrow and repentance and of intercession.

Education for Community Life

We are not individuals when it comes to our faith. While we have a personal relationship with God and often pray privately, we celebrate our faith best when we celebrate it as part of the community of the Church. In learning that they are not just individuals and must acknowledge the wider community as children become socialised, they will also learn that they are part of a wider community of faith – the class, the school, the family, the parish, the diocese and the Church as a global and Catholic community.

Missionary Initiation

Being part of this wider community of faith means becoming aware of the need of others in respect of the global family and in respect of the command of Jesus to 'Go out and make disciples of all nations'.

The children are helped to understand how the Holy Spirit has always led people to an awareness of the needs of others and to be prepared to respond to those needs,

*sometimes in courageous and far-reaching
ways. The children are led to an awareness of
the Holy Spirit's presence in their own lives,
leading them to respond similarly to the needs
of those in their own world.*[10]

Pedagogical Method

The programme follows a particular method in
helping the children learn and the key to the process
followed in the *Alive-O* programme is: focus,
explore/reflect and respond. As with most things
that children learn today it begins with the
experience of the child. The programme attempts to
form the child in a particular way and imbue them
with a particular type of knowledge:

*The kind of knowing that we seek is not only
one which leads to clarity of thought and
articulation, but one that profoundly influences
the whole of an individual's approach to life. We
seek to lead the children to become the kind of
people who see the world around them and all
that is happening in it through the eyes of faith,
and whose interpretations of what is happening
and responses to it are all influenced by their
faith.*[11]

Focus

The programme seeks to engage the children within
the limits of their childhood; their experience so far
both at home, in school and possibly in church, their
experience of the world around them, and the social
and natural environment in which they live. The
limits of their vocabulary and understanding are
also taken into consideration, but challenged where
necessary and when appropriate. The focusing on a
particular subject or theme is done through games,
stories and activities.

We take for granted much of what happens in our daily lives. Only in rare moments do we stop and think and ask questions about the significance of the ordinary events of our lives. In this religious education programme we seek to provide the opportunity for the children to do that: to stop and think; to ask questions; to explore; to wonder.[12]

Explore/Reflect

Here the children are invited to dwell on what they have heard and to explore it. This helps to increase awareness of what is being learnt. The reflection helps to evoke a sense of wonder and mystery, which is at the base of all worship, but has an important place in catechesis; otherwise the material becomes dry and barren.

We seek to provide opportunities for the children to become reflective people who will take time to stop and think, so that they will have the capacity to become aware of the presence and action of God in their lives and in the world around them.[13]

Respond

Through words and pictures, acting, singing and prayer the children learn to respond to the material that they have encountered. A variety of responses gives the teacher the opportunity to pitch the programme according to the intellectual ability, imagination and flair of the class being taught.

So, for instance, it may be that they have spent some time thinking about those at home who love them. A response might be, that they

would make a card saying 'thank you' to those people. It may be that having spent some time thinking about the wonder of the natural world, they take time to pick up litter in the school playground.[14]

Some Elements of the Programme

Story
Story forms an important part of the *Alive-O* programme.

> *Stories have the capacity to explore abstractions in terms of images and interpersonal experiences. They provide a stage peopled by characters exemplifying the great forces that have shaped humanity and where we can see love, hatred, greed, generosity, compassion and jealousy in action. A good story is a mirror, which shows us the heights and the depths of human experience, and in doing so gives us the opportunity to view our own experience at a safe distance.*[15]

The vast majority of the stories that the children hear are biblical in origin. I say in origin, because often the stories are adapted to the comprehension and interest of the children. You may remember when you and your child celebrated the Sacrament of Reconciliation for the first time. The story of the Lost Sheep from Luke 15:1-7 forms the core of that celebration, and is used in the classroom as a way of bringing the children to an understanding of the infinite love of God. In *Alive-O 3*, the story is told firstly as it appears in the Bible, next from the point of view of the lost sheep and then from the point of view of the shepherd. In *Alive-O 4* it is told from the point of view of the ninety-nine left behind.

Another example of adapting Bible stories comes in *Alive-O 7*. In a story from Acts 20: 7-12, Paul is preaching and a young man falls out a window. In the programme the young man is given a name, Eutychus, and he is used as a link in a number of the lessons in Term 3. This method appeals to the imagination of the child and to a sense of connectedness with the story.

Poetry
Poetry is a natural ally in the development of religious imagination and it can turn the account of ordinary events into something lasting and memorable.

> *The struggle to become fully alive is one that unfolds through experience and is expressed through language. In a particular way, experience and language are what poetry works with too. Without the language which poetry puts on human experience, that experience can be hollow and empty.*[16]

The successful use of image in poetry is at the heart of the best poetry. The inclusion of poems in the programme gives children the opportunity to come in contact with imagery and to learn to appreciate both its transcendence and immanence. The use of poetic imagery, may also help the development of the religious imagination of the child, and assist the child when it comes to writing prayers, or even poems of their own. Poetry here has an appeal to the senses. Apart from the aforementioned, poetry has its own rewards.

Reflect
As the children grow and learn to look at concepts and ideas, the programme offers them the opportunity of chatting, reflecting, and a call to

action. The aim is to engage the children with the teacher and with each other as regards the content of the lesson.

> *The learning process is helped by giving the children the opportunity to put words on what they are learning or experiencing. In doing so they make their own of something new or different.*[17]

It helps the teacher elucidate as to how well a topic has been understood. Conversation is a medium for learning and the children learn from the answers and opinions of other children. It is not necessarily a question and answer session, but a drawing out of the information learnt by the children, in a non-examination arena. It requires considerable patience on the part of the teacher, especially as children get more confident and speech skills become more developed.

Music

> *Music and song speak to the heart in a way that often transcends the spoken word. Music uplifts the spirit and renews the soul.*[18]

It is also great fun. The music for *Alive-O*, most of which was composed specially for the programme, is fresh, modern and well-written. It helps to explore the themes of the lesson and the spirit that should be gained from the lesson. In *Alive-O 7* and *8* there are a number of songs written for use in the preparation for and celebration of the Sacrament of Confirmation: *Spirit Anthem* helps the children to learn the symbols of the Holy Spirit; *Spirit-Filled Day* teaches the Fruits of the Holy Spirit; *Today and From Now On* teaches the Gifts of the Spirit; and another song, which in a modern and child-friendly way, teaches the Ten Commandments.

Art
As with poetry, art deals with the world of imagery.

> *More than any formal, abstract means of communication, such as language or writing, the image is the immediate personal language of the senses. In a world where many things are transitory, it alone remains as a meaningful record of an event, a sensation, an experience and an emotion. The ever-changing world of the child needs art as a means of expression. It makes possible the externalisation of what might otherwise remain a confused mass of uninterpreted, unrelated stimuli. Art allows the many stimuli – aural, sensory and emotional – to find unity in expression.*[19]

Children learn to express themselves in art and as a form of expression it is without correction or contradiction. Art is never a situation of right or wrong, although some children are better at it than others. Painting is a very reflective and silent art form and leads the children to thinking about a subject without the need for interaction or speech. As a form of contemplation it ties in very well with the contemplative aspect of prayer.

The following section will give you an insight into some of the ideas and themes of these programmes for fifth and sixth class, along with a brief introduction to each lesson. For each programme there is a pupil's book and a workbook. Children will probably have a religion copy also. There are also sheets entitled *At Home with Alive-O*, which are included in the teacher's resource pack. The suggestion is made to teachers that these sheets are sent home to parents on a number of occasions during the school year; so as to keep parents informed of the work being undertaken in class.

However, there is no substitute for getting involved in these lessons by talking to your children about what they have been doing in school relating to all these or any lessons in the *Alive-O* programme.

ALIVE-O 7

The major theme of *Alive-O 7* is spirit. In this year, children are either treating this as the first of two years of preparation for the Sacrament or are getting ready to celebrate the Sacrament of Confirmation during the year. The theme, apart from dealing with the Holy Spirit, also covers the notion of spirit in general. The power and action of the Holy Spirit is all-pervasive:

- It is evident in the practice and witness of adults in the home, in the school and in the local community.
- It is evident in the lives of the children.
- It is evident in the sacramental, liturgical and prayerful celebrations.
- It is evident through the living out of the commandments and through a love for the Word of God.
- It is the Spirit of God in Jesus who moves us to faith, hope and love in the first instance.
- The work of parent, teacher and priest in Religious Education is a work of co-operation with the Holy Spirit.
- The Holy Spirit is the source of all growth and development in faith and, as the Spirit of

Wisdom, Understanding, Knowledge and Light,
is the unseen agent in Religious Education.
• The Holy Spirit disposes us to welcome the Word
of God.

TERM 1

Lesson 1
Opening A New School Year
The year begins with a short ritual. This ritual not
only explores the importance of beginnings, of new
possibilities in our lives, but also the idea of
responding to those key moments throughout our
lives in prayer and ritual.

Lessons 2-6
Prophecy
These lessons offer an opportunity to explore prophecy
as a biblical phenomenon and the call for children to be
prophetic in their own lives. Prophecy is about insight
more than foresight. The metaphor of clay is used in
these lessons reflecting the idea of God as Potter. The
work with clay is done in a prayerful atmosphere.

Lesson 7
Mary and the Mysteries of Light
Every year in *Alive-O* there is a lesson on Mary, the
Mother of God. This lesson explores the five
recently introduced *Luminous Mysteries* or
Mysteries of Light, encouraging us to meditate on
certain particularly significant moments in Christ's
public ministry: Jesus' Baptism in the Jordan; Jesus'
self-manifestation at the Wedding at Cana; Jesus'
proclamation of the Kingdom of God, with his call
to conversion; Jesus' transfiguration; Jesus'
institution of the Eucharist, as the sacramental
expression of the paschal mystery.

Lesson 8
The Saints
As with previous *Alive-O* programmes, the children are introduced to two Irish saints – Saints Laurence O'Toole and Kevin. The former was canonised by the Church and the latter was declared a saint by '*vox popularum*' (the voice of the people), due to the devotion that grew up around the saint. The children are also introduced to icons and their use in prayer.

Lesson 9
The Garden Story
The story of the Garden of Eden is not to be taken literally. It is a symbolic story, which is an attempt to explain the human condition and the circumstances of the human race – we are born in a state of separation and alienation from God, and that God continues to love us in spite of our sin.

Lessons 10-11
The Commandments
Moses has been covered in nearly all the *Alive-O* programmes. The Commandments are seen in the context of God's unconditional love for each of us and are presented both in traditional and modern way. Other types of commandments from the New Testament are mentioned – the *Kingdom commandments*, and the *Our Father commandments*.

Lessons 12-14
Waiting In Joyful Hope
These lessons in Advent offer the children an opportunity to experience 'waiting in the spirit of Advent.' The key characters of the lesson are Isaiah, John the Baptist and Mary.

TERM 2 AND 3

Term 2, Lessons 1-5
The Seamless Garment
Using the metaphor of weaving, the children are introduced to an exploration of the Christian call to grow and develop in an holistic way and to their full potential. The weaving activity central to the lessons aims to reinforce the notion of a unity of a life despite the various colours, strands and fabrics encountered. Creating this unity in the fabric of life is the Spirit of unity. The lessons concentrate on the Christian Faith, Christian Community, Christian Morality and Christian Love.

Term 2, Lessons 6, 12 and Term 3, Lesson 1
Lent, Holy Week and Easter
Lesson 6 focuses on Lent as a time for new beginnings, new growth – a time to get fit for the climax of Easter and to live the life of a Christian. Lent invites us to a change of heart, to a change of lifestyle. In lesson 12 the saving actions of Jesus Christ, which are the events of Holy Week, are recalled. The concentration is on Palm Sunday – Jesus' entry into Jerusalem; Holy Thursday – Washing of the Feet; and Good Friday – The Passion Narrative. The first lesson of term 3 concentrates on four post-Resurrection events: Women at the Tomb; Jesus and Thomas; Jesus appearing to the seven disciples; The Emmaus story.

Term 2, Lessons 7-11 and Term 3, Lessons 3-6
Sacrament of Confirmation
There are a number of lessons relating to the Sacrament of Confirmation. Three are completed by Confirmation and Non-Confirmation classes; two by Confirmation classes only. These lessons are

done before Easter or before the Confirmation ceremony. After Easter (or Confirmation) there are four lessons that are titled 'Where Do We Go From Here'. These four lessons are meant to offer the children a way of engaging with the spirit, history and heritage of the early Christian Church. They are taught through means of a drama, meant to deepen the children's understanding of growing as a Christian after Easter or Confirmation.

The lessons in preparation for the sacrament will deal with the symbols, gifts and fruits of the Holy Spirit. Connections are made with the other Sacraments of Initiation – Baptism and Eucharist. It is important to ask for, to hope for, to desire the coming of the Holy Spirit. Such desire is met with a new breath of life, bestowing good news for people of all ages: good news about the love of God. The Rite of Confirmation is studied along with the history of the sacrament. The role of sponsors is explained along with information on choosing a Confirmation name.

Provision has been made in the lessons for a 'parish link'. Ideally, this material will be used by parish personnel, for example, a priest, catechist or parish team, in order that the local faith community will be given an opportunity to support the children in a very real, public way. Hopefully, parish personnel will take the initiative as regards the Parish Link material. If the class teacher wishes to be engaged in this process, the parish will surely welcome such co-operation.

Term 3, Lesson 2
The Risen Jesus is Present at Mass
In every year since *Alive-O 3* there have been lessons relating to the Eucharist. This lesson focuses on the presence of the Risen Jesus: Under the appearance of

bread and wine, the body and blood of Christ; in the body of believers in Jesus, the body of Christ; In the Word, broken and shared for our nourishment, in the celebrant and other ministers, sharing through Baptism and Holy Orders in the Priesthood of Christ.

ALIVE-O 8

The major theme of *Alive-O 8* is creative relationship. In all aspects of life we are 'in relation'. From early in the *Alive-O* programme the children have learnt that they are not alone, in terms of their family, the community, the school and the Church. They have learnt that they form part of these communities and that there are certain ways of acting within these groups; certain responsibilities and obviously certain rules and regulations involved with these relationships. These human relationships are explored in this year's programme. The term 'creative relationship' has been chosen very carefully to signify the types of relationship that we can have as human beings. You and I are friends: sometimes we are very close; sometimes not; we argue, we laugh and perhaps cry; we learn from one another; we are a support and an influence on one another. That which exists between us is a creativity and an energy that can bind us together as friends. Rather than speaking about 'good' or 'bad' relationships, the term 'creative' can suggest a great deal more of what can exist between two people, groups of people, members of a particular parish, the boys and girls in a class and their teacher; the list of definitions for creative relationships is infinite. The potential of relationships in our lives and the lives of those around is something that can be life-giving and that will hopefully bring out the best and most creative in us.

The programme doesn't just confine itself to an exploration of the aspects of human relationship. The children explore relationship in terms of the world around them – to the world of science, to the natural world, to ecology and to the environment. The third and most significant aspect of relationship that is explored in this programme is our relationship with the Risen Jesus, which happens through the sacraments.

This programme also contains a significant amount of material relating to the Sacrament of Confirmation. This will be the second year that material has been done relating to the sacrament. The reason for this is two-fold: firstly, some children will receive Confirmation in fifth class and some in sixth; secondly is the desire that children are introduced to the material for the preparation and celebration of Confirmation over a two-year period. You may remember that something similar happened when the children received the Sacrament of Reconciliation and made their First Holy Communion.

TERM 1

Lessons 1 – 6
In Relation
In this set of six lessons the theme of creative relationship is explored. It is done here through exploring our relationship with the natural world, with the world of language, mathematics, science and in the area of human relationships. The ultimate and most perfect example of creative relationship is that of the Blessed Trinity. *The Catechism of the Catholic Church* says: 'Christians are baptised in the name of the Father and of the Son and of the Holy Spirit. Before receiving the sacrament, they respond to a three-part question when asked to confess the

Father, the Son and the Spirit: "I do". The faith of all Christians rests on the Trinity CCC 232,' and 'the Trinity is a mystery of faith in the strict sense, one of the mysteries that are hidden in God, which can never be known unless they are revealed by God' CCC 237. The Trinity is a difficult and complex mystery, which has occupied the minds of theologians for millennia. In the programme, by speaking of the Trinity in the terms of creative relationship, the children are able to explore the Trinity in a manner that is appropriate to their young age and faith.

Lessons 7 – 12
Sacraments and Sacramentality

In this series of lessons, the children are introduced to the general idea of the sacraments and their meaning. From the beginning of the *Alive-O* programme, the children have been introduced to ritual as an integral part of responding to the material that they have been learning. The Word of God has also been an important part of the programme, and they are familiar with the idea of gathering as a community, either as a parish community or as a class or school community. Further exploring the role of gathering, symbol, ritual and word in terms of the sacraments, helps to develop an appreciation of sacramental reality, which differs from, but is grounded in the life that we live. In two specific lessons, the seven sacraments are covered. In the first lesson, the sacraments of Baptism, Eucharist, Confirmation, Reconciliation and the Anointing of the Sick are revised. They have been previously covered in other *Alive-O* programmes. In the second lesson, they are introduced to the Sacraments of Marriage and Holy Orders.

Lessons 13-16
Nativity Play
In the lessons that are taught during Advent, the children learn through a drama. Advent and Christmas has been covered throughout the entire previous seven years of the programme, and the children are familiar with the idea of watching and waiting, of preparation and anticipation, which is the central theme of Advent for the Christian Church. The theme of the drama is 'Word': the relationship between the Word of God as found in the scriptures and the 'Word Made Flesh' – the Son of God, who 'lived among us'.

TERM 2 AND 3

Term 2, Lessons 1 – 5
Confirmation
These lessons are offered as preparation for the celebration of the Sacrament of Confirmation and build on the work that has been done in *Alive-O* 7. Lessons 1-3 concentrate on the 'call to witness', which is an implicit part of the Sacraments of Baptism and Confirmation. The story of Pentecost is the story of a community emerging from the upper room to be the heralds of the Good News of Jesus Christ, a mandate that is given to each of us. Lessons 4-5 are the same as those in *Alive-O* 7. As with *Alive-O* 7, there are a series of Rituals that are offered for celebration in the parish, so that the community can become involved, through ritual and prayer, with the preparation for the Sacrament of Confirmation.

Term 2, Lesson 6
Mary
In this lesson, the presence of the Holy Spirit in Mary is explored, especially in the great prayer of

Mary, the Magnificat, from the gospel of St Luke. The children learn about some of the various feasts associated with Our Lady.

Term 2, Lessons 7 – 8 and Term 3 Lesson 1
Lent, Holy Week, and Easter
These lessons are part of the exploration of the liturgical year, which form an important part of the *Alive-O* programme. In *Alive-O* 3, Jesus is described as a journeyman. Journey is one of the great themes of human history and a common theme in literature and in the scriptures. Jesus as journeyman is the man who never stayed still, always going from one place to another; a command he subsequently gave to the seventy-two disciples when he sent them out to preach his word, 'when he sent them out ahead of him, to all the places he himself was to visit' (Luke 10:1). In the seasons of Holy Week and Easter, all Jesus' journeys come to a culmination, with Jesus' journey to Jerusalem and his Passion and Death, and his journeying with his disciples after the Resurrection, as he prepares to leave them.

In lesson 7 the link between the celebration of the season of Lent and the preparation for Baptism is explored. In the Early Church, the season of Lent was the last part of the journey of catechumens before their initiation into the Church on Holy Saturday night, at the Easter Vigil. Lesson 8 follows some of the events of Holy Week, told through the eyes of the centurion Longinus. Longinus, according to legend, was the soldier who pierced Jesus' side with a lance, and he was said to have become a Christian. He is commemorated in a statue in St Peter's Basilica in Rome. Longinus narrates the journey of Jesus to the cross, from the entry into Jerusalem, the clearing of the Temple, the capture of Jesus in the Garden of Gethsemane, and the crucifixion of Jesus. The first lesson in term 3 stays with the character of Longinus, as he narrates the journey of Easter from the Resurrection to the coming of the Holy Spirit at Pentecost, and it includes some of the post-Resurrection appearances of Jesus.

Term 3, Lessons 2 – 8
The Kingdom of God
These final lessons of *Alive-O* 8 and indeed, the whole *Alive-O* programme are concerned with the Kingdom of God. The kingdom is seen in terms of 'right relationship' or 'creative relationship' of all the elements involved. Jesus revealed the Kingdom of God as that which constantly empowers the world with the possibility of good. The Kingdom of God has already been explored in *Alive-O* 5, when the children learnt of the Kingdom of God in the presence and actions of Jesus. In the lessons here the Kingdom is seen: in the relationship between the various parts of the body; the relationship between children; the relationship of power and poverty in the developing world and need for social justice; the relationship between the various Christian Churches; the relationship with the environment and our caring for creation; the relationship with the Kingdom when it arrives 'in the fullness of time'.

Lesson 3 contains material that is normally part of the Relationship and Sexuality Education in Primary Schools. Here it is presented in the context of the Kingdom of God. The lesson follows the five dimensions of the body mentioned in the Social Personal and Health Education (SPHE) programme: breathing, feeding, growing, reproducing and sensing. It should be remembered that Relationship and Sexuality Education (RSE) should be the responsibility of both parents and teachers, in conjunction with the school authorities. Whereas the material is offered, it is advised that it should be taught in accordance with the RSE policy of the school's Board of Management, and should not be undertaken without the permission of parents. None of this material appears in the pupil book.

Chapter 2

The Holy Spirit

There is a story that St Augustine was walking along the seashore one day contemplating the mystery of the Trinity. As he was walking, he noticed a boy pouring a bucket of water into a hole he had dug. 'What are you doing?' asked Augustine. 'I'm going to empty the sea into this hole,' replied the boy. 'You'll never get the whole ocean into that hole,' said Augustine. 'And you,' replied the boy 'will never get the mystery of the Trinity into your mind.'

Hardly a true story, but one with the essence of the dilemma of anyone faced with trying to explain the mystery of the Trinity, or more specifically in this case, the Holy Spirit. It is far easier to look for evidence of the Holy Spirit than to attempt to define the Holy Spirit.

The Holy Spirit is the third person of the Trinity and 'is at work with the Father and the Son from the beginning to the completion of the plan for our salvation' *Catechism of the Catholic Church* 686. At Baptism we are baptised in the name of the Father and of the Son, and of the Holy Spirit. In the simplest of terms the Father creates, the Son redeems and the Holy Spirit inspires. We believe in one God in three persons – Father, Son and Spirit. They are distinct as persons, and are relative to one another. The Holy Spirit is God's loving presence in each person and in the community if the Church, and the fulfilment of the promise of Jesus to send his Spirit to be with us always.

In life there are many things that we find hard to describe, and it is easier for us to offer images as an explanation. It is much easier to show examples of the many different types of love that exist than to give an all-encompassing definition of love. The evidence of faith and hope is far easier to show and talk about than trying to attempt a satisfactory explanation. With the Holy Spirit, it is perhaps easier to speak about the action of the Spirit than about the Spirit, and with the Holy Spirit we begin not with the early Church, but with the genesis of life.

In the Hebrew Scriptures

We have a tendency to think of the Holy Spirit in terms of the Christian Church, but the evidence of the power and working of the Spirit is contained in the Hebrew Scriptures. At the beginning of creation we hear that the 'Spirit of God was moving over the face of the waters,' in the first chapter of Genesis. The Spirit is evident in the work and words of the prophets. Isaiah speaks of the working of the Spirit in the successor to David:

There shall come forth a shoot from the stump of Jesse, and a branch shall grow out of his roots. And the Spirit of the Lord shall rest on him, the spirit of wisdom and understanding, the spirit of counsel and might, the spirit of knowledge and fear of the Lord. And his delight shall be in the fear of the Lord. Isaiah 11:1-3.

40

and in the prophet Ezekiel:

> *A new heart I will give you, and a new spirit I will put within you; and I will take out of your flesh the heart of stone and give you a heart of flesh. And I will put my spirit within you, and cause you to walk in my statutes and be careful to observe my ordinances. Ezekiel 36:26*

In the New Testament

The presence of the Spirit begins with the Annunciation of the birth of Jesus and the angel telling Joseph that Mary was with child 'by the Holy Spirit'. After his Baptism in the Jordan the Spirit descended on Jesus in the form of a dove. The Baptism in the Jordan is one of the few stories of Jesus that is recounted by all four of the evangelists. Later, St Luke gives an account of Jesus' testimony in the synagogue at Nazareth. It occurs after his temptation in the wilderness, and as his public ministry is beginning. He stands up in the synagogue and reads from the scroll of the prophet Isaiah:

> *The Spirit of the Lord is upon me, because he has anointed me to preach good news to the poor. He has sent me to proclaim release to the captives and recovering of sight to the blind, to set at liberty those who are oppressed, to proclaim the acceptable year of the Lord. Luke 4:18-19*

Throughout the Gospels we hear phrases like 'filled with the Spirit...' and 'Jesus was led by the Spirit...' It is testament to the power of the Spirit working in the life and ministry of Jesus. At the end

You will receive power when the Holy Spirit comes on you, and then you will be my witnesses not only in Jerusalem but also throughout Judea and Samaria, and indeed to the ends of the earth.

Acts 1:8

of this earthly ministry, Jesus promised that he would not leave his followers orphaned.

> *When the day of Pentecost had come, they were all together in one place. And suddenly a sound came from heaven like the rush of a mighty wind, and it filled the entire house where they were sitting. And there appeared to them tongues as of fire, distributed and resting on each one of them. And they were all filled with the Holy Spirit and began to speak in other tongues, as the Spirit gave them utterance.*
> *Acts of the Apostles 2:1-4*

In Luke 3:16, John the Baptist had spoken about a Baptism of the Holy Spirit and fire. The account goes on to list the various people who were in Jerusalem at that time. In an act that seems to reverse the story of the Tower of Babel, the Apostles burst out from the room and began to preach to these various peoples, each of them in their own native language. At the tower of Babel, language had been fragmented and communication lost. Now with Pentecost, the Spirit brought unity and understanding. The people gathered in the room had been fearful after the departure of Jesus, now they were ready to take up the ministry for which he had chosen them. Then Peter begins to speak:

> *Men of Judea and all who dwell in Jerusalem, let this be known to you, and give ear to my words. For these men are not drunk, as you suppose, since it is only the third hour of the day; but this is what was spoken by the prophet Joel: 'And in the last days it shall be, God declares, that I will pour out my Spirit upon all flesh, and your sons and your daughters shall*

prophesy, and your young men shall see visions,
and your old men shall dream dreams; yea, and
on my menservants and my maidservants in
those days I will pour out my Spirit; and they
shall prophesy ... And it shall be that whoever
calls on the name of the Lord shall be saved.'
Acts 2:14-19, 21

The Acts of the Apostles continues with many
references to the Holy Spirit. Philip is moved by the
Spirit to convert the Ethiopian in Acts 8:29. Peter
converts the first gentile, Cornelius a Roman
centurion, along with his household in Acts 10:1-48.

In the Life of the Church
From the beginning of the life of the Church and the
baptism of Cornelius, the power of Jesus was open to
all. The significance of the words 'all flesh' in Peter's
speech at Pentecost is that the spirit is not just
poured out on a chosen few, but on all people, which
is where we come in. From the very beginning the
Church has relied on the power of the Spirit working
through the followers of Jesus. The astonishing and
dramatic events of Pentecost should not distract us
from the significance of the events. Concentrating on
what happened at Pentecost might make it seem
foreign to our own personal faith experience, and as
a result could make the coming of the Holy Spirit on
us seem insignificant. Recounting the story of
Pentecost is not about how the Holy Spirit was
poured out on the Apostles, but that it happened and
changed them completely. It is the same for the
followers of Jesus today. The Holy Spirit is poured
out on us at our Baptism and the fullness of the Holy
Spirit given to us in Confirmation, which also
changes us completely.

Great Paraclete to
thee we cry,
O highest gift of God
most high
O fount of life, O fire
of love,
And sweet anointing
from above.

S. Webbe & E. Caswell
*(Come O Creator
Spirit Blest)*

We call Pentecost the birth of the Church and the Holy Spirit has called each successive generation of Christians to the community of faith in a manner similar to that recounted by the evangelist Luke after the story of Pentecost:

And they devoted themselves to the apostles' teaching and fellowship, to the breaking of bread and the prayers... And all who believed were together and had all things in common; and they sold their possessions and goods and distributed them to all, as any had need. And day by day, attending the temple together and breaking bread in their homes, they partook of food with glad and generous hearts, praising God and having favour with all the people. And the Lord added to their number day by day those who were being saved.
Acts 2: 42, 44-47

The Church is the Body of Christ and the Temple of the Holy Spirit. In the Church the mission of Jesus is brought to completion. This early community gathered for the breaking of bread, they held everything in common, and they gave generously to the poor. It may seem like a long way off from the Church of today, but evidence of that early Church is still in the Church today. As a Christian community we gather to celebrate the presence of the Risen Jesus in the Eucharist, in obedience to the command of Jesus to 'do this in memory of me'. As a community of faith we are encouraged to give to the poor, perhaps not in the way the early Church did, by selling off everything we have and holding all things in common, but we can't fail to be encouraged by the frequent generosity of people.

Even in the early Church, Christians were people who attempted to live a message in the world, which was out of this world. While going about their daily lives in the present world they were anchored in the hope of the world to come. Through the centuries the Church has been affected by the world around it, sometimes to the good, sometimes not. The Church has been influenced by social doctrine, new philosophies, the sciences, by art and by literature. It has led to the rise of people of great courage; witnesses to the power of the Holy Spirit. The Church in its members and collectively has been capable of great acts of courage, dignity, creativity, generosity, and all that the Spirit can do to prompt the hearts and souls of its members. It has also seen the visible signs of its humanity and ability to sin, in the actions of the Church as an institution and by individual members. Much has been done in its name, which has been a source of shame and sorrow. The Holy Spirit constantly calls the Church to renewal and to a new Pentecost, to become rededicated to the preaching of the gospel, and to the breaking of bread.

Father of light, from whom every good gift comes,
send your Spirit into our lives
with the power of a mighty wind,
and by the flame of your wisdom
open the horizons of our minds.

Opening Prayer from the Solemnity of Pentecost – *Roman Missal*

SYMBOLS OF HOLY SPIRIT

A symbol is not just a representation of something; it encapsulates more than that. A flag is not just the symbol of a country. It can be the symbol of national pride at a football match or on a national holiday; a symbol of a nation's grief when laid on a coffin; a symbol of defiance in times of persecution. When speaking about the Holy Spirit, the Church offers a number of symbols. In relation to Confirmation, reference is usually made to three:

Wind, Breath and Fire. The Catechism of the Catholic Church also names among others associated with Confirmation: Water, Anointing, Cloud, Light, Seal, Hand, Finger and Dove. CCC 694-701

Wind: On the day of Pentecost the Holy Spirit first seemed to appear as a mighty wind. The wind is a powerful symbol of what was to happen next. The power of the Spirit gave the followers of Jesus the strength to preach the Good News of Christ risen. Throughout the history of the Church men and women, prompted by the Spirit have brought change to the Church and the power of the mighty wind is still felt today in the Church's work of social justice, in debt relief, and in the preaching of the Gospel.

Breath: In one of his last appearances to the Apostles before the Ascension, Jesus came to them and breathed on them saying 'receive the Holy Spirit' John 20:22. Long before that, God had created Adam out of clay and breathed life into him. During the Chrism Mass when the oil of Chrism is being consecrated, the Bishop breathes and in the prayer of consecration says: 'Pour out the gifts of your Holy Spirit on our brothers and sisters who will be anointed with it. Let the splendour of holiness shine on the world from every place and thing signed with this oil.'

Fire: We speak of the tongues of fire that descended on the Apostles at Pentecost, which reminds us of the Baptism of the Holy Spirit and Fire promised by John the Baptist. Fire signifies the transforming energy of the Holy Spirit; it burns and purifies. As the prayer says: Come Holy Spirit, fill the hearts of your faithful. Enkindle in them the fire of your love. Send forth your Spirit and we shall be created, and you shall renew the face of the earth.

The Gift of the Holy Spirit

Any parent knows that children love to receive gifts. When they do, they don't open it neatly and tidily, storing the wrapping paper for use later. Children rip. The anticipation with which they expect a gift at Christmas or for birthdays and the excitement that they have in receiving a gift is one of the delights of childhood. This is how it could be with the gift of the Holy Spirit. It is a gift to be used, not stored away. This is not the type of treasure that Jesus told us to store up (Matt. 7:19). We see the gift of the Holy Spirit as the power and possibility of action in the life of the young person being confirmed and by extension the possibility of action in the life of the community of the people of God, the Church.

In the Confirmation ceremony the Bishop prays, asking God to:

Send the Holy Spirit to be their to be their helper and guide.
Give them the spirit of wisdom and understanding,
the spirit of right judgement and courage,
the spirit of knowledge and reverence,
Fill them with the spirit of wonder and awe in your presence.

and he anoints the candidate with the words, *Be Sealed with the Gift of the Holy Spirit.*

Many of you will remember learning the seven gifts or the seven-fold gift of the Holy Spirit off by heart before your own Confirmation. Here's a reminder.

Wisdom

In the Hebrew Scripture, God offered Solomon any gift he could want. He chose wisdom. The gift is about the possibility of seeing things as God sees them. It is the gift to look at life with a different perspective – the perspective of faith. It is the possibility of knowing how to live a good life and striving to do that. It is about listening to the voice of the spirit in our heart and acting on those promptings.

Understanding

It is easy to learn facts and figures, dates and places. The gift of understanding is the possibility to give meaning to what we learn through wisdom. On the road to Emmaus, the disciples met the Risen Jesus. Having explained everything that had happened in Jerusalem and why they were downcast, Jesus set out to explain everything in the scriptures about himself. The disciples knew the facts, Jesus helped them understand and make sense of those facts.

Right Judgement

The world in which young people inhabit today calls for this part of the gift of the Holy Spirit more than anything else. They are bombarded with a myriad of choices and tempting alternatives. The gift of right judgement is the possibility of making the right choices in life, according to Christian values, and sometimes despite what our friends, society, or culture would have them believe is the right choice.

48

Courage

Coming closely on the previous part of the gift of the Holy Spirit is the courage to handle the consequences of Right Judgement. The gift of courage is the possibility to make the right choice even though we would rather go with the crowd, or follow the latest trends, the current fashions, and the will of the peer group. Young people today are not likely to be called to the courage of martyrdom as in the early Christian Community, but it can be inordinately difficult to stand up for your beliefs, or to take a stand against something you feel is wrong.

Knowledge

While not dissimilar to Wisdom and Understanding, the gift of Knowledge helps us to know about our faith and about the world. We often talk about making an informed decision about something and the Holy Spirit helps in the gaining of that knowledge. The gift requires a contribution on our part – we cannot know about the world just by divine inspiration. It requires effort on our part, but we have the possibility of the help of the Holy Spirit.

Reverence

Traditionally this part of the gift of the Holy Spirit is about how we act religiously; blessing ourselves passing a Church, genuflecting, a sense of reverence when going to receive Holy Communion. It is still all these things, but it can mean much more. In interpreting this gift as reverence for all God's creation we acknowledge the possibility of the respect and reverence for the environment, we acknowledge the reverence due to every person we meet, who like us are children of God and 'a temple of the Holy Spirit'.

Wonder and Awe in God's Presence

Traditionally this was the part of the gift know as fear of the Lord. Wonder and Awe in God's Presence sums it up better. It is the gift that helps us to see the work of God in the ordinary and extraordinary ways. It is an acknowledgement of the power of God working through our lives, through the lives of others around us, through the Church and through creation. 'Consider the lilies of the field, how they grow; they neither toil nor spin; yet I tell you, even Solomon in all his glory was not arrayed like one of these.' (Matt. 6:28-29)

The Fruit of the Holy Spirit

An image that is often used with the Gifts and Fruits of the Holy Spirit is that of the tree. The gifts of the Holy Spirit are the roots of the tree, and the fruits of the Holy Spirit are, the fruits of the tree. If we are led by the Spirit and open to God's gifts, the fruits of the Holy Spirit will be evident in our lives and in this way people will see that the Holy Spirit is active in our lives, in our work, in the way we treat others and in the way we serve the community of the Church as the practical living out of the gift of the Holy Spirit given at Confirmation. The fruit of the Holy Spirit is mentioned by St Paul in his letter to the Galatians 5:22 as the virtues of love, joy, peace, patience, kindness, goodness, faithfulness, gentleness and self-control. Paul sees the fruit of the Holy Spirit as the counterbalance for the various vices. The gifts and fruits of the Spirit are also alluded to in the second letter to the Corinthians 6:6, in the letter to the Colossians 3: 12-15 and in the letter to the Ephesians 4:2, 5:9. In the *Alive-O* programme the fruits of the Holy Spirit are described as follows:

Love – the Spirit lives!
Joy – the Spirit dances!
Peace – the Spirit rests!
Patience – the Spirit waits!
Kindness – the Spirit gives!
Goodness – the Spirit moves!
Gentleness - the Spirit acts!
Faithfulness – the Spirit dwells!
Self-Control – the Spirit smiles!

Here are some of the many scripture references that can be linked to the Fruit of the Holy Spirit:

Love: 'Love is always patient and kind; it is never jealous; love is never boastful or conceited; it is never rude or selfish; it does not take offence and is not resentful. Love takes no pleasure in other people's sins but delights in the truth; it is always ready to excuse, to trust, to hope, and to endure whatever comes. Love does not come to an end.' *1 Corinthians 13:4-7*

Joy: 'With gratitude in your hearts sing psalms, hymns and inspired songs to God; and never say or do anything except in the name of the Lord Jesus, giving thanks to God the Father through him.' *Colossians 3:16-17*

Peace: 'Peace I leave with you; my peace I give to you; not as the world gives do I give to you. Let not your hearts be troubled, neither let them be afraid.' *John 14:27*

Patience: 'There is no need to worry; but if there is anything you need, pray for it, asking God for it with prayer and thanksgiving, and that peace of God, which is so much greater than we can understand, will guard your hearts and your thoughts, in Christ Jesus.' *Philippians 4:6*

Kindness: 'You are God's chosen race, his saints; he loves you and you should be clothed in sincere compassion, in kindness and humility, gentleness and patience.' *Colossians 3:12*

Goodness: 'Share your food with the hungry and open your homes to the homeless poor. Give clothes to those who have nothing to wear, and do not refuse to help your own relatives. Then my favour will shine on you like the morning sun.' *Isaiah 58:7-8*

Faithfulness: 'I pray not only for these, but for those also who through their words will believe in me. May they all be one Father, may they be one in us, as you are in me and I am in you, so that the world may believe it was you who sent me.' *John 17:20-21*

Gentleness: 'I, the prisoner in the Lord, implore you to lead a life worthy of your vocation. Bear with one another charitably, in complete selflessness, gentleness and patience. Do all you can to preserve the unity of the Spirit by the peace that binds you together.' *Ephesians 4:1-2*

Self-control: 'Finally, fill your minds with everything that is true, everything that

is noble, everything that is good and pure, everything that we love and honour, and everything that can be thought virtuous or worthy of praise.'
Philippians 4:8

Chapter 3

The Sacrament of Confirmation

Some initial thoughts on sacrament would be a good place to begin. I have already mentioned how it has been treated in the *Alive-O* programme, but some further comment is required. The word sacrament comes from the Latin *sacramentum*. In the ancient Roman world it signified a pledge of money or property which was deposited in a temple by parties to a lawsuit or contract, and which was forfeited by one or other if the suit was lost or the contract broken. The word also came to mean the oath of allegiance that soldiers took to both their commanders and to the gods of Rome. It had therefore a religious or sacred significance. In the second century, Christian writers used the word to describe Christian Initiation – in that Baptism was like a *sacramentum* administered to 'new recruits', and marking their new life in service of God and the Christian community. As the Roman Empire began to decline the word remained in usage in the Church and came not only to signify Baptism, but also any blessing, liturgical feast, or holy object.

The word *sacrament* signifies a hidden reality: it is a sign of something that is sacred or mysterious. It is sacred in the sense that it is precious or important, and mysterious in that it is not fully understood. Every religion has things that it signifies as sacred, as sacramental. There are sacred places like temples, churches, shrines, mountains; there are sacred actions like prayer, chanting, singing, blessing, fasting, gestures; there are sacred objects like vessels, pictures, icons, statues, vestments, writings; there are sacred persons like priests, sacrificial victims, kings and queens, prophets, holy men and women, shamans, gurus. To untrained eyes and without initiation into the mysteries and sacred rituals of any religion, all these are just a collection of things, places and people. For believers they are sacred because they signify something beyond themselves, something special, and something that is hidden and mysterious.

We are quite familiar with all the signs that surround us in everyday life: road signs giving us directions and regulating our speed; signs that tell us when a house is for sale or when there's twenty per cent off. Logos are one of the great signs of the modern age. Everyone can identify brand logos and labels, especially children. Any parent, who has struggled with a child's desire or demand for a certain type of trainer, can empathise. These signs communicate a direct emphatic message. In our religion we have certain signs, with which we are all familiar and to which we show deference and respect. A symbol is a special sign, which helps give expression to experiences and meanings, which often defy language: we all like cake, and it's nice to treat ourselves from time to time. However, put candles on it and it signifies something more. Put twenty-one, forty, fifty, or even one hundred candles and then the significance is even greater;

The Sacraments are efficacious signs of grace, instituted by Christ and entrusted to the Church, by which divine life is dispensed to us. The visible rites by which the sacraments are celebrated signify and make present the graces proper to each sacrament. They bear fruit in those who receive them with the required dispositions.

Catechism of the Catholic Church 1131

sunsets happen every evening without fail, but sit and watch it with someone special, or at the end of an eventful day, perhaps after eating some of the cake with the candles, and it has an even greater meaning; rings are just bands of gold, silver, or a base metal, but offer and exchange them as part of a celebration of the sacrament of marriage and they have a whole new meaning, which often cannot be put into words. For the people living in the ancient world of the Roman Empire, the cross was a means of execution. To Christians it becomes the symbol of redemption, the triumph of Christ over sin and death. Water is one of the basic things needed to sustain life. Bless it and pour it over the head of a baby and it becomes something that sustains more than just physical life.

Theologian Joseph Martos calls sacraments 'doors to the sacred', invitations to religious experiences. The anthropologist Mircea Eliade calls them 'hierophanies' from the Greek words, '*hieros*' meaning sacred or holy, and '*phaino*', meaning to manifest or reveal. Therefore, a sacrament is a manifestation of the sacred.[1] This experience of sacrament is the experience of entering a place where space, time and meaning are sacred. One of the elements of the *Alive-O* programme has been to encourage the teacher to create a 'sacred space' in the classroom. This has been a very successful addition to the liturgical and spiritual formation of the children. With the addition of religious images like statues and icons, and liturgical symbols like candles and crucifixes, it has helped to evoke an attitude of prayer and to focus the prayertime in class. One teacher told me that as soon as she lights the class candle at the beginning of prayertime, the children have an awareness of a different moment of time in the school day. In the classroom space, time and meaning can become sacred.

It wasn't until the twelfth century that the number of sacraments was restricted to the seven that we have today. The *Catechism of the Catholic Church* describes these seven sacraments as: 'powers that come forth from the Body of Christ, which is ever-living and life-giving. They are the actions of the Holy Spirit at work in his Body, the Church. They are the 'masterworks of God' in the new and everlasting covenant' CCC 1116. The celebration of the sacraments, according to the theologian Bernard Cooke:

> *was the celebration of those ultimate 'mysteries' that had been revealed in the life and death and resurrection of Jesus of Nazareth. Sacramental liturgies brought men and women into a world beyond the purely human, into the realm of the sacred, into contact with divine power and, it was hoped, divine mercy and grace ... While these mystery celebrations were intended to worship and acknowledge God, they were also meant to benefit the humans who performed them... For the past thousand years or so, this understanding has taken the form of belief that salvation came to people through sacraments; sacraments 'give grace.' They overcome human sinfulness; they give men, women, and children the moral strength to lead good lives and so reach their destiny; they bring people closer to God.[2]*

The sacraments transform us, but this can only be achieved by an active participation on our part. 'The sacraments are efficacious signs of grace, instituted by Christ and entrusted to the Church, by which divine life is dispensed to us. The visible rites by which the

The Sacrament of Confirmation confers a character. By it the baptised continue their path of Christian initiation. They are enriched with the gift of the Holy Spirit, and are more closely linked to the Church. They are made strong and more firmly obliged by word and deed to witness to Christ and to spread and defend the faith.

Canon 879
Code of Canon Law

sacraments are celebrated signify and make present the graces proper to each sacrament. They bear fruit in those who receive them with the required dispositions' CCC 1131. Sacraments don't just happen to us as we stand on the sidelines as a passive or partly interested spectator.

Finally it must be remembered that the celebration of a sacrament is not just about the individual. When we all gather and celebrate a birthday, we all benefit from the event. At times of sadness we can all be moved in some way and in varying degrees. In the celebration of the sacraments: 'the fruit of sacramental life is both personal and ecclesial. For every one of the faithful on the one hand, this fruit is life for God in Christ Jesus; for the Church, on the other, it is an increase in charity and in her mission of witness' CCC 1134.

HISTORY OF CONFIRMATION

If people in the Early Christian Community wanted to commit themselves as followers of Christ, they had to be baptised with water. Sometimes those people also received the 'laying on of hands' from leaders in the Christian Community, or they were anointed with oil, that is, they were marked with consecrated oil as Christians. Today the laying on of hands and anointing are the central actions of the Confirmation ceremony. Scholars, however, cannot establish whether this laying on of hands and anointing with oil in the New Testament had anything to do with what we now call Confirmation. There is no clear evidence of a separate sacrament of Confirmation at this time in the history of the Church.

58

Gradually, the ceremonies that signified a person was becoming a Christian became more elaborate and involved. At first, solemn initiation (the process of becoming a member of a group) into the Church took place in a single ceremony. That ceremony normally unfolded during the Easter Vigil service. After a long period of instruction that sometimes lasted as long as three years, each candidate was baptised individually and apart from the main assembly, and then clothed in a white garment. The candidates were then brought before the Bishop, the leader of the local church, and the other members of the assembly. The Bishop laid his hands on the candidates; he prayed that the candidates might receive the gift of the Holy Spirit. From the fourth century, bishops have used the prayer that we currently use in the Confirmation ceremony today.

After a time, because the number of those who wanted to be Christians grew so quickly, the Bishops were no longer able to be present at every ceremony of initiation. The Eastern Church, that is, the Churches in what we now call the Middle East, resolved this problem by allowing priests to administer the whole ceremony of initiation. To this day in many Eastern Churches, the ceremony of initiation remains a single ceremony. So, a person is baptised, 'confirmed', and shares in the Eucharist in the course of one ceremony, even if that person is an infant.

In the Western Church, the Church of Rome, the problem was resolved in quite a different way. The ceremony of initiation was divided into separate ceremonies that took place at different times. Priests were allowed to baptise and it seems that most often they gave Holy Communion in that ceremony, too. However, bishops alone could lay on hands and anoint. Bishops completed the initiation process in this way whenever they could arrange to be present in a particular area.

We are not quite sure why the Western Church chose this means of resolving the problem. We do know that when this division of the ceremony of initiation took place, people began to think in terms of two different or separate sacraments: Baptism and what came to be called Confirmation.

Over the course of the next few centuries, Confirmation became more and more separated from Baptism, both in time and in meaning. Christians no longer saw it clearly as the sealing or completion of Baptism. They began to look upon it in many different ways; as a sacrament of growth, or of maturity, or of commitment. Only at this time did the idea of Confirmation making a person a 'Soldier of Christ' arise and gain support.

Chronology

Although, as stated, there was no clear emergence of Confirmation as a separate sacrament until after the third century, the elements of the Sacrament of Confirmation can be recognised in the Sacrament of Baptism in the early Church.

30 - 100 AD   After Pentecost, the Apostles began initiating new members into the Christian community. These procedures were loosely organised, but followed closely the practices used in the Jewish groups at the time. Procedures included a period of preparation, comprising of instruction and repentance. This was followed by reception into the community through a bath of water and sometimes a laying on of hands.

200   Later a longer period of preparation was required. This included instruction, prayer, fasting, repentance and good works. A Sponsor was also required to present a candidate to become a Catechumen (one under instruction). Preparation could last up to three years under of the care of the Sponsor who witnessed to the moral quality of the Catechumen's life.

    At Baptism, each catechumen went into the water where they were asked to state their belief in Jesus Christ. Up to three immersions took place. Deaconesses assisted the women during this ceremony. After Baptism, the bishop anointed each person on the forehead to signify being joined with Jesus Christ. Then the bishop greeted each with the kiss of peace.

300   Later, more rituals, for example, breathing on the candidate to blow away evil spirits and blow in the Holy Spirit, were added to the form of the sacraments. Special places were built apart from the church as fitting places for driving out devils (Baptisteries). With the growing number of Baptisms and churches, bishops were no longer able to preside at each Baptism to confirm it by laying on of hands. Hence, Baptism and Confirmation began to emerge as separate ceremonies. Confirmation took place whenever the Bishop could be present.

500	Only as Christianity became the prevailing religion did infant Baptism become the common practise. Hence the period of preparation no longer seemed necessary. In some places, Confirmation continued to immediately follow Baptism. During the Middle Ages, fifteen was the usual age for Confirmation, but practises varied widely.
1565	The Council of Trent stated the age of reason to be sometime between the ages of seven and eleven.
1789	After the French Revolution, twelve was considered the more appropriate age for Confirmation. The bishop's kiss of peace now became a token blow on the cheek to signify that one must be ready to suffer for Christ.
1962	The Second Vatican Council prepared new guidelines for the sacraments of Baptism and Confirmation. The latter is now seen in terms of initiation and generally takes place within the Eucharist. Before being confirmed, candidates renew their Baptismal Promises, are next confirmed and then celebrate and receive the Eucharist. Thereby they enact again the traditional initiation sequence of Baptism, Confirmation and Eucharist. The new rites of Confirmation were introduced in 1971.

CEREMONY OF CONFIRMATION

Introduction
On the day of your child's baptism you brought them to the church and began their journey of faith. You stood before the priest and the community of the Church, represented by your family and friends and promised to 'keep the flame of faith alive in their hearts' (Rite of Baptism). You promised 'to be the first teachers of your child in the ways of faith' (Rite of Baptism) and also to be 'the best of teachers' (Rite of Baptism). Over the last twelve years you have been responsible for teaching them their prayers, bringing them to Church, giving them the first lessons in right and wrong. The family is described as the 'domestic church' (*Lumen Gentium 11*), where your children receive their 'first Christian experience' (*General Directory for Catechesis* 226), and this experience 'frequently leaves decisive traces which last throughout life' GDC 226.

On the day of Confirmation it is time for children to take on the responsibility for their own faith. In many parishes a Service of Light is held some time before the Confirmation ceremony. I have heard parents say that they found this a more memorable occasion, when compared with the hustle and bustle that often accompanies the Confirmation day. During this ritual, parents light again the candle that was first lit on the day of their child's baptism and they then hand that candle to their son or daughter. The ritual symbolises the handing on the responsibility for their faith to the child. However, for parents and godparents it is not the end. Parents still have a great deal to do with the religious upbringing of their children, a responsibility which often remains throughout life.

Father,
you have made this mixture of oil and perfume
a sign and source of your blessing.
Let the splendour of holiness shine on the world
from every person signed with this oil

Second Prayer for Consecration of Chrism – *Roman Missal*

Almighty God,
Father of your Christ,
your only-begotten
Son,
grant me a spotless
body, a pure heart,
a watchful spirit, a
knowledge without
error.
Let the Holy Spirit
come
so that I may possess
the truth and believe
it firmly
though your Christ.
Through him, glory to
you,
in the Holy Spirit for
ever! Amen

Prayer of the
Confirmed Person
from the Apostolic
Constitutions (c.380)

Parents will always pray for their children, and hopefully in a spirit of love and caring offer advice and encouragement from time to time.

On the day of Confirmation the school is also present with the teachers, the choir, the servers and all the others is takes to celebrate the Sacrament of Confirmation. The teachers that are present have prepared the young people in the last year for the Sacrament of Confirmation. However, on the day they also represent the many teachers who have nurtured the faith of the boys and girls over the years since they began school, because teachers 'have the responsibility to cultivate this gift by nourishing it and helping it to grow' GDC 244. It is the special function of the school to 'enable young people, while developing their own personality, to grow at the same time in that new life which has been given to them in baptism' GDC 259.

On the day of Confirmation the Christian community is present once again. The community of the particular parish plays its part in the journey of faith of the young people who are about to be confirmed. By virtue of their own Confirmation, the members of the community 'are more perfectly bound to the Church and are endowed with the special strength of the Holy Spirit. Hence they are, as true witnesses of Christ, more strictly obliged to spread the faith by word and deed' (*Lumen Gentium 11*) 'The parish is, without doubt, the most important place in which the Christian community is formed and expressed. It is the place where faith is born and grows' GDC 257. All who help in the preparation for the day of Confirmation have helped the faith of candidates. In the words of St Paul 'I received from the Lord, what I also delivered to you' 1Cor. 11:23. It is the privilege of the community to contribute what was contributed for them – the witness, prayer and practical assistance to the young people. In the future and in their turn the girls and boys who are confirmed today will help the future generations.

Finally the clergy are present – the bishop and the priests of the parish. The bishop is the original minister of Confirmation. The reason for this is to signify an obvious link with the coming of the Holy Spirit on the Apostles at Pentecost. As the leaders of the Church, the bishops are the successors to the Apostles. In certain circumstances the bishop may delegate the parish priest or another priest as an extraordinary minister of the sacrament, most usually the parish priest of the parish where the sacrament is taking place.

In the normal course of events the celebration of the Sacrament of Confirmation takes place during the celebration of the Eucharist. Confirmation (like Baptism) is connected with the Eucharist. The Gift of the Holy Spirit confirms us as children of God and brothers and sisters of Jesus Christ, uniting ourselves more consciously with Jesus, who offers to the Father his sacrifice of love for the salvation of the world. The word 'Eucharist' means thanksgiving. The Gift of the Holy Spirit makes us more aware of the goodness of God and deepens our sense of gratitude and thanksgiving. The Holy Spirit teaches us to address God as 'Father' Gal. 4:6. Finally, the Holy Spirit, the Spirit of Jesus enables us to appreciate more fully that partaking with others in the Bread of Life at Communion commits us to a life of mutual love and sharing in accordance with the commandment of Jesus: 'love one another'.

Ordinarily there is a sponsor with the child. The choice of sponsor very much depends on the local custom. Many times it is one or other parent or both, sometimes a child's godparent, sometimes an

The rite of Confirmation is to be revised in order that the intimate connection of this sacrament with the whole of Christian initiation may stand out more clearly.

Constitution on the Sacred Liturgy, 71

older brother or sister. The criteria for a sponsor is that they are confirmed themselves, are Catholic and in good standing.

The ceremony of Confirmation is in four parts: Presentation of the Candidates; Renewal of Baptismal Promises; The Laying on of Hands; Anointing with Chrism.

Presentation of the Candidates

After the Gospel the bishops and the priests take their seats. The parish priest or his delegate will present the candidates for Confirmation. The candidates are asked to stand and present themselves for receipt of the sacrament. This presentation of candidates is also part of the rite of ordination for a priest and bishop. It marks the willingness of the candidates to go forward and receive the sacrament that is about to be conferred on them. They stand up by themselves in marked contrast to the day when they were carried to the Church on the occasion of their baptism. In some places and depending on numbers, the names of the candidates are read out. Sometimes the bishop asks the parish priest about the preparation that has been undertaken by the candidates before Confirmation. The parish priest usually gives a brief description of the faith journey of candidates up and until the present time.

Renewal of the Baptismal Promises

After a homily by the bishop, the young people are asked to stand to renew the promises made for them at Baptism by their parents and godparents. In Baptism we became children of God, followers of Jesus Christ, and members of the Church. In Confirmation we publicly profess our faith in God our Father and in Jesus Christ who sent us the

Spirit to enable us to take part in the life and mission of the Church.

Laying on of Hands

The laying on of hands is the biblical gesture by which the Holy Spirit in invoked. In Acts 6:1-7, the Apostles lay their hands on the seven they chose to assist them. In Acts 13 the prophets and teachers of the Church at Antioch laid their hands on Paul and Barnabas before they undertook the particular ministry for which God was calling them. The laying on of hands is used in Confirmation and in other sacraments. In Confirmation it evokes the invisible gift of the Holy Spirit given to us by God. The bishop accompanied by the priests present lay their hands on the children for Confirmation during the prayer: It begins with the bishop saying:

My dear friends, in baptism God our Father gave the birth of eternal life to his chosen sons and daughters. Let us pray to our Father that he will pour out the Holy Spirit to strengthen his sons and daughters with this gift and anoint them to be more like Christ, the Son of God.

Pause and all pray in silence. The bishop and priests extend their hands over the candidates

All-powerful God,
Father of our Lord Jesus Christ,
by water and the Holy Spirit
you freed your sons and daughters from sin
and gave them new life.
Send your Holy Spirit upon them
to be their helper and guide.
Give them the spirit of wisdom and understanding,
the spirit of right judgement and courage,

The second sacrament is Confirmation, whose matter is chrism blessed by a Bishop. It is made from oil, which consciously signifies excellence, and balsam, which signifies the aroma of good character. And the form is, 'I sign you with the sign of the cross, and I confirm you with the chrism of salvation. In the name of the Father and of the Son, and of the Holy Spirit.'

Council of Florence, 224 (1439)

the spirit of knowledge and reverence.
Fill them with the spirit of wonder and awe
in your presence.
We ask this through Christ our Lord. Amen

Anointing with Chrism

The sacramental sign of Confirmation is the anointing with Chrism and the words 'Be sealed with the gift of the Holy Spirit.' This anointing is a sign that our whole being has been filled by the power of the Spirit. The oil used for this anointing is Chrism. Chrism is used in the sacraments of Baptism, Confirmation and Holy Orders: the head of the newly-baptised is anointed with chrism, the forehead of the person confirmed, the head and hands of a bishop at his consecration, and the hands of a priest at his ordination. It is used in the consecration of churches, chalices, patens, altars and altar-stones.

The word 'chrism', comes from the Greek *'chrisma'*, and was used to designate any substance used for the purposes of smearing or anointing, such as the various kinds of oils, unguents, and pigments. Eventually its meaning was restricted to oil used in religious functions and ceremonies. It is a mixture of purest olive oil and balsam. There are many references in the Hebrew Scriptures to the use of oil in religious ceremonies. It was used in the coronation of kings, in the consecration of the high priest and in the ordination of the Levites. Balsam is an aromatic, resinous substance that is extracted from the wood of certain trees or plants. In the beginning the Christian Era it was obtained from Judea and from Arabia, but today it comes from the West Indies. Chrism is blessed by a bishop in a special manner at the Chrism Mass. Rather than making the sign of the cross over it, as with other blessings, the Bishop breathes on it, signifying the invocation of the Holy Spirit.

As the person is anointed during the Confirmation ceremony, the Bishop say, 'Be sealed with the Gift of the Holy Spirit'. This gesture and the words accompanying it express clearly the effects of the giving of the Holy Spirit. Signed with the perfumed oil, the young person receives the seal of the Lord and the gift of the Holy Spirit, drawing them closer to Christ and to the ministry for which all, as baptised Christians, are called.

Chapter 4

Other Perspectives on the Sacrament of Confirmation

A constant protest heard by religious educators is that children aren't learning the way their parents and grandparents learnt in their day. The problem is that children today are not living in the same world as their parents and grandparents did. As a reminder of that world of our parents and grandparents, I offer this quotation from Louise Fuller, writing in *Irish Catholicism since 1950*:

> *A good barometer as to the state of Irish Catholic culture in the early 1950s is the summary of a report to the Congress of the Lay Apostolate, made in Rome, on 10 October 1951, by Very Rev. M. O'Halloran, administrator of City Quay parish, Dublin. Referring to the state of Irish Catholicism, he pointed out that 'we are living in an atmosphere steeped in Faith'. He went on to express satisfaction with the fact that the Church in Ireland had almost complete control of the systems of education, explaining that this was one of the reasons why the Irish parliament*

was almost one hundred percent Catholic in thought and action. This, according to O'Halloran, was also why trade unions were not Communistic or anti-clerical, why there existed close relations between people and clergy, and why there were so many vocations for the Church. He pointed out that the numbers who attended daily Mass and Holy Communion and weekly confessions were 'remarkably high and can hardly be repeated anywhere in the world', and he added that 'a priest or nun is more than welcome in any and every house, rich or poor, at any hour'. All in all, he opined, 'it would seem we are in a very happy position.'[1]

God is the giver of all life, human and divine. May he bless the father of this child. He and his wife will be the first teachers of their child in the ways of faith. May they also be the best of teachers, bearing witness to the faith by what they say and do, in Christ Jesus, our Lord

Blessing of Fathers –
Rite of Baptism

Today we are not in that position. Change has happened at a speed unprecedented in the history of civilisation and with the rapid change over the last fifty years, and even more so over the last twenty years, the challenge of handing on the faith is greater than it ever was. In fact it is a monumental task, and we can no longer rely on the methodology that succeeded in the past. As a means towards an explanation, let me offer a story:

Back in pre-historic times, there was once a tribe who lived at the edge of a forest and beside a river. They survived by hunting and fishing and they lived a happy and secure life. With their clubs, they hunted the small woolly horses that lived in the forest and they fished by grabbing the fish out of the pools and streams of the river. Their only predator was the sabre-tooth tiger, which they frightened away with the use of fire. One of the tribesmen, who was known as a thinker, saw that the combination of these three activities gave the tribe security and nourishment. He realised that to maintain this security, the young men of the tribe needed to be taught these three activities. So for many generations young men were taught horse-clubbing, fish-grabbing and tiger-scaring and the tribe prospered and possessed enough meat, skins and security. The heart of a good education lay in the three subjects.

Many generations later an ice age began to make its presence felt. A great glacier began to move down from the mountains to the north. Year after year the glacier got nearer and nearer. As it did, the debris from the glacier was deposited in the river. The river became muddy and it was difficult to see the riverbed. As the glacier moved through the forest, it made the ground wet and marshy and the horses moved further south where the ground was easier underfoot. Antelopes came in their place. There was a positive note: the sabre-tooth tiger also found it too cold and moved south. However, the tiger was replaced by bears, who were not afraid of fire.

There was a crisis in the tribe. Even those who were acknowledged experts failed to catch fish, scare bears or hunt antelopes. The tribe were starving and dying. Some radical young men and women had begun to learn and experiment with new techniques. They had developed a crude fishing net, which they lowered into the water and were able to catch fish. Others had begun to hunt the antelope with spears and were having some success. Others had thought of a way to catch bears with a bear-pit, and also had some success. The elders of the tribe were horrified at these younger members of the tribe. Had they no respect for the traditions of the tribe? Had they no respect for the wisdom and learning that had served the tribe so well in the past and would serve it well again? They and all belonging to them were banished and sent to live elsewhere. Many years later members of this new tribe, which had grown large, went to search for the old tribe. They searched the area where the old tribe had lived – by the forest, near the river – but there was no one left. The tribe had become extinct.[2]

In order for us to survive and be nourished, the curriculum has to change; sometimes to stay the same, things have to change. That is not to say that the central truths of our faith are not important. The central truths of our faith are essential to help our faith grow and develop, so that it will have an effect our lives and in the lives of all with whom we come in contact. However, the means by which these truths are taught will change as pedagogical methods change, as society changes, as children change.

Firstly, in a section called 'The Changing Child', I offer some brief and general theological and sociological perspectives on the changing notion of childhood, as it is found in this time in history and at this time of sacramental preparation. Secondly, in the section entitled 'The Emerging Adolescent' I talk about the interaction between psychological development of the young adult and preparation for the sacrament, especially in relation to the community in which they live and practise their faith. Finally, I mention a number of peripherals to the preparation and celebration of the sacrament: drugs and alcohol, and the day of Confirmation itself and the money and presents associated with it.

The Changing Child
The sacrament of confirmation is an important stage in the life of the young person. It confirms what was begun at Baptism. In their preparation they reflect

on some of the changes that are happening to them in the context of the wider world, beginning with the Christian community in which they live. The preparation also reflects some of the changes and attitudes in their own minds and hearts (and indeed bodies). It opens them to an awareness of the Holy Spirit which was given to them at Baptism and which is a help to them in this time of change and growth.

Let me state categorically that I am not making a case for Confirmation on the basis that the children are at some particular stage of psychological development. While we should acknowledge the psychological development that occurs around the time of Confirmation, it is important to emphasise that sacramental initiation is not undertaken just for the reason of fulfilling a 'rite of passage'. This is like saying that just because they are a certain age or in a certain class in school that they should be confirmed. Confirmation is not a Bar Mitzvah or Bat Mitzvah. There is no declaration 'today I am a man/woman' after the celebration of the sacrament. Confirmation is not about puberty, adolescence, or any other stage in human maturity. Confirmation is more than that. Confirmation celebrates the gift of the Holy Spirit that is shared in the faith community, and is present in the lives of these children, as an integral aspect of their life in Christ.

The great twentieth-century theologian Karl Rahner was one of the few theologians of the modern era, or indeed any era to offer a contribution on how children should be seen theologically, or of what a theology of childhood should consist. In 1977 he published his most famous essay on the subject, *Ideas for a Theology of Childhood*. [3]

Rahner outlines his thoughts on a number of issues relating to childhood. His opening remarks state the 'unique and unrepeatable value attached to childhood'.[4] He suggests that human beings think in terms of stages of life, and in thinking in this way, are prone to the idea that one stage is preparation for another: meaning when a stage is over, it no longer has value. The stages of youth and childhood are mostly envisaged in this manner; that when we grow up, childhood disappears. He specifically blames Christianity for developing this subordinate role for childhood. Children were seen as being under the control of their parents, teachers and clergy in a form of passive obedience, just as their parents were under the control of clergy and hierarchy in a similar form of passive obedience, and the sooner children grew up and became 'paying, praying and obeying' adults, the better. Rahner is attempting to put the idea of stages in life in its proper context. It is a means to an end, not an end in itself. He states: 'It is obvious that human life goes through not only biological phases and stages of development, but also spiritual ones as well, and that man's being a body-spirit means that the two of course go together. Each of these phases has its own special stamp, its own irreplaceable character, its own unique significance, its own particular weight, and no other phase can be a substitute for it. And all of them build up together, reaching out through their successors, towards the consummation, which lies beyond our empirical reach, of a complete and resurrected human being'.[5] For Rahner, phases or stages of life are only one part of the picture. A human being is the sum of past, present and future, all of which is redeemed. As humans go forward, they retain the past and head towards a future that they have worked out in freedom. Rahner says that what is true of every other stage of life is true of childhood also.

Childhood then is not a stage through which we must pass in order to 'graduate' into adulthood. It is not something passing or past, but part of the totality of our existence, the 'single and enduring completeness of the time of our existence considered as a unity'.[6] In this way, childhood always remains open to us, an existence in which we remain living, long after the chronological childhood has passed, and we move towards the eternity of childhood. Rahner sees childhood as the field where only certain things can grow, ripen and bear fruit, and 'be carried into the storehouses of eternity.'[7] Childhood in these terms has a value in itself; precious 'not merely because it seeks the riches of life in its maturity. The strange and wonderful flowers of childhood are already fruits in themselves, and do not merely rely for their justification on the fruit that is to come afterwards. The grace of childhood is not merely the pledge of the grace of adulthood.'[8] For Rahner, childhood is openness, infinite openness and the mature childhood of an adult is the maintenance of that openness. This is the openness that allows the development of our relationship to the Infinite. Childhood has as much to contribute to the life and faith of the Church as any other stage of growth.

Many historians, sociologists and anthropologists have tried to explain the function of childhood. One of the most obvious functions is socialisation. Children learn as they grow that they are part of a wider group that has rules and regulations to maintain the order of the group. This begins with the home, the class and the school, and children learn to take their place as part of society. It is a gradual learning process, and as the child grows they are eventually initiated into the world of the adult. One of the tasks of adulthood was to eventually initiate children into this world when the time was appropriate. The 'knowledge gap' that existed between what children knew and what adults knew was successfully maintained for centuries until the arrival of new forms of media. With television and the Internet, children are often able to find out about things without the help of their parents. When children are doing this in an environment that is not monitored problems arise. On the one hand children may be exposed to all sorts of information, images and other material without the intellectual or emotional ability to process it. As the knowledge gap begins to collapse, so does adult authority. In a superb book on the death of culture entitled *Lost Icons – Reflections on Cultural Bereavement,* the Archbishop of Canterbury Rowan Williams, laments the death of the notion and the actuality of childhood in our age. 'There is a particular horror and pathos in children not – as we say – *allowed* to be children'.[9] He is in favour of the prolonged 'latency' of the human young, which is not only a function of the biological vulnerability of infancy, but also has to do with how human beings perceive themselves. He sees a necessity for childhood so that children can be in an environment that allows them to make mistakes, to act foolishly, to play and to learn to develop and control their use of language.

Rowan Williams goes on: 'The perception of the child as consumer is clearly more dominant than it was a few decades ago. The child is the (usually vicarious) purchaser of any number of graded and variegated packages – that is, of goods designed to stimulate further consumer desires... If the child is a consumer, the child is an economic subject – even if someone else actually provides the cash, the demand is the child's.'[10] Television plays an early and important part in learning this consumption mentality: pre-schoolers watch an average of twenty-seven hours per week. One of the principle techniques for hooking children into commercial products is the sale of toys featured as the main characters of children's television programs.

Richard Louv sums up the future of childhood in North America better than I. What goes for North America goes for the rest of the developed world: 'Today's children are living a childhood of firsts. They are the first day-care generation; the first truly multicultural generation; the first generation to grow up in the electronic bubble, the environment defined by computers and formed by television; the first post-sexual revolution generation; the first generation for which nature is more of abstraction than reality; the first generation to grow up in new kinds of dispersed, deconcentrated cities, not quite urban, rural, or suburban. The combined force of these changes produces a seemingly unstoppable dynamic process: childhood today is defined by the expansion of experience and the contraction of positive adult contact. Each part of this process feeds and speeds the other. The more of the manmade world that children experience, the more they assume they know (and as they become teenagers, the less they think they need adults). Because children seem to know more about the world, adults are more likely to assume, sometimes wishfully, that kids can take care of themselves. As a result, children and adults pass each other in the night at ever-accelerating speeds, and the American social environment becomes lonely for both'.[11]

The Emerging Adolescent

Childhood and later adolescence is marked by the continuing search for identity. Our identity comes from what we bring from our past and what we hope to achieve and be in the future. Young people have a hand in forging their own identity. The use of the image of the 'forge' by the psychologist Erik Erikson gives us insight into the type of struggle that takes place in identity search. A great deal is hammered into shape. The young person is looking beyond the family and towards society, searching for new signs of identity. Identity becomes formed through the opinions of people outside the family. Adults form an important part of the identity struggle, sometimes in the form of parents, sometimes in the form of mentors. Parents may no longer be the only guides. There are others whose advice and encouragement young people can also value: teachers, clergy, scoutmasters, sports coaches, or the old lady next door: sometimes anyone other than their parents. These people may offer an ideology that differs from the parent.

At the time of Confirmation, children can be preparing to leave the safe, secure environment of primary school to enter into the mysterious world of second-level education. Added to this are the various other fears that they have for their future: fear of failure, of not finding their place in life, of not finding friendship. As they grow up, young people need to find reasons to express and ultimately live a particular faith and its value system, as opposed to all the others that are offered to them by society or the prevailing culture. They need to find a voice to express all that troubles and concerns them. Young people are not necessarily looking for the answers; they want the ability, the freedom, and the safe environment to ask the questions. In the words of Rainer Maria Rilke, they need to 'learn to love the questions'.[12] The questioning, philosophising, teasing out that children do needs to have expression. They need to make sense of what they perceive their faith is, rather than just adopting the total system of values and beliefs of their parents. The catechesis that we undertake in preparing for Confirmation can offer a context for young people to talk about their faith and how it affects their lives. *The General Directory for Catechesis* outlines the effectiveness of this type of catechesis: 'The most successful catechesis is that which is given in the context of the wider pastoral care of young people, especially when it addresses the problems affecting their lives. Hence, catechesis should be integrated with certain procedures, such as analysis of situations, attention to human sciences and education, the co-operation of the laity and of young people themselves' GDC 184. For young people these are the 'gang' years: a realisation of the value of the group. The young person feels the need for solidarity and acceptance among their peers. 'They are sometimes morbidly, often curiously, preoccupied with what they appear to be in the eyes of others as compared with what they feel they are.'[13] In sacramental preparation, there exists the possibility of tapping into the group dynamic as a means to explore and discuss issues, although caution must be exercised. Firstly, there is a danger of isolating anyone who doesn't feel part of the group. Young people have a harrowing ability to isolate and marginalise, and this would have a detrimental effect on a sacramental program. Secondly, within a group discussion of faith, there is a danger that reactions to issues discussed become group opinions, without any personal resonance in the lives of these young people. Cathal gives an opinion of who he thinks God is, and Eve and some of the rest of the group agree. Has Eve sacrificed an authentic opinion of God, for the sake of conformity with the group?

Just as they see the value in their small 'gangs' or groups, so young people begin to take notice of the wider group of the Christian Community. In the preparation for Confirmation, they become more aware of their growing role and responsibility as members of the Christian community. They may also begin to see themselves as part of the wider society. This awareness should be reciprocated through the awareness and acknowledgement of these children by the wider Christian community. This community has a responsibility to offer them support in their growth, the witness of a life of faith worth living, and guidance toward and along the path of life. After all, as mentioned previously, the celebration of the Sacrament of Confirmation in a parish is a celebration of the whole assembly gathered in faith. In the preparation for Confirmation, understanding community in a spiritual sense is important; understanding it in a psychological sense is vital. Our faith is expressed in community, and accepting a particular faith is correlated with membership in the community of faith. It is a constant challenge to a community of faith to see people who claim to hold and profess a particular faith, without becoming a member of that community. Being a member, and preferably a participating member of a particular faith community is not something that can be taught. Again it is something that must be experienced. The whole preparation for the sacrament should be a time for the children being confirmed to be drawn closer into the faith life of the community, a life based on the Spirit. The question for the community is not only about what is to happen in the lives of these children about to be confirmed. The question is what will happen to the community as the gift of the Holy Spirit is poured out on the whole community. It is not about what these young people will contribute to the faith life of the community, but how the contribution that they are making at the present will be greatly enhanced by the action of the Holy Spirit.

Finally, it is not about what these young people can do for the community, but what the community will do for them. They will be adult members eventually. At the moment they are adolescent or young members and we should not be excessive in expectation, but generous in offering our encouragement, prayer and support. Perhaps it would be an idea that, as the children undertake their course of instruction to prepare for the sacrament, the parish could likewise undertake their own course of instruction to help the children in their preparation, and more importantly to become more conscious of their own awareness of and response to the work of the Holy Spirit in their lives. I am not suggesting that parishioners would have to attend evening classes or endless meetings, but that the Sunday Eucharist could become a place of catechesis for the entire parish community in the months and weeks leading up to the celebration of Confirmation. All liturgies associated with the preparation of the Sacrament of Confirmation should take place within the context of the Sunday Eucharist, giving the celebration of the Sacrament of Confirmation back to the community. These young people come from our community. It is only right and proper that the preparation and celebration of the Sacrament should be part of the faith expression of the community. There is no better way to give witness to, and celebrate the presence of God in our community and in young people. Furthermore, for the Sundays leading up to the celebration of Confirmation, the children should be included in the

Prayer of the Faithful. Through the prayer and worship of the parish community, we give witness of the life of faith that we hope they will aspire to, because the prayer and worship of a parish community are not simply consequences of faith. They are the building blocks of faith.

Alcohol and Drugs

For many years one of the parts of the Confirmation ceremony was the taking of the Pledge. It usually happened towards the end of the ceremony and in some ways it was the first sign of the newly confirmed child coming to terms with standing on their own two feet and making a decision for themselves. For young people it was often a very important promise and was often combined with membership of the Pioneer Total Abstinence Association. Others, of course did not take the Pledge, or did not keep the promise implied in it, for whatever reason. Over the last number of years some bishops have opted to remove the taking of the Pledge from the Confirmation ceremony. The reason for this is to heighten awareness of the importance of the pledge. In other words, rather than the Pledge being almost an appendix to the ceremony, it was removed and given a place and an importance as part of the preparation for the Sacrament. An addition to the Pledge concerning alcohol were the promises made regarding drugs, which were obviously not an issue in our grandparents' day, but are most certainly an issue today.

Much of the talk about Confirmation revolves around the gift or gifts of the Holy Spirit. In life we are offered a wide variety of other gifts: the talents God gives us to use wisely and well for the sake of the Kingdom of God; the gifts of good friends and family; the gift of health; the gift of education. As with all gifts these are appreciated, opened up and used. We all remember, in the Parable of the Talents, what happened to the man who went and buried the talents and didn't put them to work. Alcohol is another of God's gifts, but one that has to be used wisely and appropriately.[14]

The following statistics come from the Health Promotion Unit in the Department of Health and Children from the Health Behaviour in School-Aged Children survey of 2002 and the National Health and Lifestyle Surveys, 2003, which was a joint project of the Department of Health and Children and the Centre for Health Promotion Studies, National University of Ireland, Galway.

Percentage of children who have had an alcoholic drink:

Age	Boys	Girls
10 - 11 years	41	24
12 - 14 years	55	46
15 - 17 years	84	82

Percentage of children who have had a drink in the last month ('current' drinkers):

Age	Boys	Girls
10 - 11 years	6	2
12 - 14 years	13	10
15 - 17 years	54	49

Percentage of children who had ever been 'really drunk':

Age	Boys	Girls
10 - 11 years	6	3
12 - 14 years	19	14
15 - 17 years	60	54

The following statistics make for some troubling reading:

- Per capita alcohol consumption is up 49% over the period 1989-2001 (11.4 litres of pure alcohol per capita in 2001).
- Alcohol intake is a factor in 40% of all fatal road accidents in Ireland and in 30% of all road accidents.
- 35% of sexually active teenagers say alcohol is a factor in their engaging in sex.
- Sexually transmitted infections have increased by 165% in the last decade, with 8,900 cases reported in 2000 alone.
- 48% of all criminal offences are alcohol-related. This includes 88% of public order offences, 48% of offences against the person and 54% of all criminal damage offences. These refer only to offences committed by adults.
- Over the 5-year period, 1996-2001, public order offences alone have increased from 16,384 to 42,754.
- 370% increase in intoxication in public places by underage drinkers since 1996.
- One in four (25%) of those attending hospital A & E (Casualty) departments have an alcohol-related injury/illness. One in eight (13%) present in a state of clinical intoxication.
- 26% of male and 11% of female first admissions to psychiatric services are for alcohol-related conditions (1999 figures).

- 30% of all male patients and 8% of female patients in an Irish general hospital were found to have an underlying and unidentified alcohol abuse or dependency problem.
- 34% of those seeking legal advice due to marital breakdown cite alcohol as the main cause of their marital problems.
- The economic cost of alcohol-related problems in Ireland was roughly €2.37 billion in 1999 (1.7% of GDP). This figure encompassed healthcare costs, accidents, crime, absenteeism, transfer payments and lost taxes. It represents 60% of the total revenue from alcohol to the Exchequer for that year.

The Government website is full of the results of surveys, studies and all sorts of other information about the problems of alcohol abuse and teenage drinking. It is a serious and pressing issue for all concerned.

Equally serious is the rise of a drug culture in Ireland. The addition of promises regarding drugs to the Pledge a number of years ago is testament to this. For a long time many people perceived drugs as an urban problem. Regrettably, drugs are everywhere now. There are many Internet sites for parents to find out about drugs. One of the best to access concerning drugs in Ireland is *www.drugsinfo.ie*. For parents who may not have web access there is a pamphlet available *A Parent's Guide to Drugs* from the Health Promotion Unit of the Department of Health and Children.

Before you decide to never let your child outside the door again, consider this time of preparation as an opportunity for you to talk to your children about alcohol and drugs. This is a hard thing for parents to do, as it might lead them to consider the way they treat alcohol and drugs themselves: their own drinking and smoking habits. In other words there is little point in encouraging your children to have a sensible approach to alcohol and its consumption if they saw you fall in drunk from the pub last Saturday, or you making a fool of yourself at the last family gathering. Furthermore, any training, information or advice given in school can be undermined by what they may see at home concerning alcohol. The preparation for Confirmation gives parents an opportunity to talk honestly and openly to their children about these problems.

The Day
After all the preparation, you and your child have finally reached the day of Confirmation. Often there is a great deal of anticipation and excitement leading up to the day. The day itself is the culmination of years of effort on the part of the children and a great deal of credit goes to their teachers for all that they have done for them. A great deal of credit must also go to you as a parent, who in keeping the promise made by you at their Baptism, have brought them thus far on the journey. Months of preparation by a school and a parish go into the day. Everyone wants everything to be right: choirs are rehearsed, the flowers look wonderful, the altar servers are on their best behaviour, and usual someone is running around like a headless chicken with the final few things that need to be done. The theologian Peter Fink talks about the three languages of a liturgy: the reflective language of theology, the language of song, prayer, and proclamation and the language of space, movement and interaction. On the morning of Confirmation we can hear these three languages speaking to us as we participate in the celebration and provided that

Parents are the primary educators in the faith. Together with them, especially in certain cultures, all members of the family play an active part in the education of the younger members… The family as a locus of catechesis has a unique privilege: transmitting the Gospel by rooting it in the context of profound human values.

General Directory for Catechesis, 255

the believer is properly prepared for and open to what the ritual speaks and accomplishes.'[2] These three languages do not just begin to speak at the moment the opening hymn begins on the morning of Confirmation. It begins with the adolescent coming forward; willing and open to the possibility of grace, and it continues with the journey of faith that carries on long after the final hymn has been sung on that particular morning.

There are a lot of peripherals that have become part and parcel of the traditions around Confirmation in Ireland. It is a day of celebration, and naturally as Irish people we tend to celebrate in a particular way. However, celebrating the Sacrament of Confirmation by sitting in a pub for the entire day is hardly going to stand out as a memorable experience for the child whose Confirmation day it is. One of the saddest sights I ever saw was a little girl in her First Holy Communion dress, helping a drunken parent home after closing time. Try to include your child in the decisions about how the day should be celebrated. Usually their expectations for the day are not excessive. Some want to have all the cousins and friends around; some want to go to a hotel; some want to head for a family day out somewhere. You will never, of course, hear a child say that they want to sit in the corner of a pub all day. One of the dying rituals of Irish family life is the family meal. In the busy world we live in, often members of a family eat at different times; celebrating Confirmation could be one of those rare opportunities where several generations of a family get the opportunity to sit down together and enjoy the great event, giving thanks to God for the blessings of the days, thereby mirroring the Eucharistic celebration that had happened earlier.

A teacher told me recently that the average amount of money given to children at the time of Confirmation was between €800 and €1000. This is a huge amount of money for an eleven- or twelve-year-old. I was told recently of a child, living in a prosperous area, who accumulated what was close to the 'deposit for a small house' on the occasion of their Confirmation. These are the times were living in, and there is nothing much that we can do to stop this. I would hate to have to say to a child on their Confirmation, that I was delighted for them on their big day, and had made a donation in their name to a charity. Parents will know more than I will ever know about teaching their children to manage money wisely, but in terms of their Confirmation, there is something that can be done. Children should be encouraged to give some of what they have received to a charity; perhaps they could buy a Trócaire Global Gift to help children in the developing world, or sponsor an animal with the ISPCA or Bóthar. Often schools will organise something like this for their pupils, so that they can see that the generosity that has been shown to them, can be shown to others by them. You can also ask friends and family to be reasonable and somewhat restrained in giving the children gifts. Perhaps much of this is trying to command the tide to go out, but it is something that needs to be considered. I certainly do not begrudge children the gifts that they are offered, but as St Benedict says: in all things, moderation.

Prayers for the Year

I. PRAYERS FOR EVERY DAY

The Sign of the Cross
In the name of the Father, and of the Son, and of the Holy Spirit. Amen.

Comhartha na Croise
In ainm an Athar, agus an Mhic, agus an Spioraid Naoimh. Áiméan.

Our Father
Our Father who art in heaven
Hallowed be thy name.
Thy kingdom come,
Thy will be done
On earth as it is in heaven.
Give us this day our daily bread
And forgive us our trespasses
As we forgive those who trespass against us.
And lead us not into temptation
But deliver us from evil. Amen.

An Phaidir
Ár nAthair atá ar neamh,
Go naofar d'ainm,
Go dtaga do ríocht,
Go ndéantar do thoil ar an talamh
Mar a dhéantar ar neamh.
Ár n-arán laethúil tabhair dúinn inniu,
Agus maith dúinn ár bhfiacha,
Mar a mhaithimidne dár bhféichiúna féin,
Agus ná lig sinn i gcathú,
Ach saor sinn ó olc. Áiméan.

Hail Mary
Hail Mary, full of grace,
The Lord is with thee.
Blessed art thou among women
And blessed is the fruit of thy womb, Jesus.
Holy Mary, mother of God,
Pray for us sinners,
Now, and at the hour of our death. Amen.

Sé do Bheatha, a Mhuire
Sé do bheatha, a Mhuire,
Atá lán de ghrásta,
Tá an Tiarna leat.
Is beannaithe thú idir mhná,
Agus is beannaithe toradh do bhroinne, Íosa.
A Naomh Mhuire, a mháthair Dé,
Guigh orainn, na peacaigh,
Anois agus ar uair ár mbáis. Áiméan.

Glory be to the Father
Glory be to the Father,
And to the Son,
And to the Holy Spirit;
As it was in the beginning,
Is now and ever shall be,
World without end. Amen.

Glóir don Athair

Glóir don Athair,
Agus don Mhac,
Agus don Spiorad Naomh.
Mar a bhí ó thús,
Mar atá anois,
Mar a bheas go brách,
Le saol na saol. Áiméan.

Morning Prayer

Father in heaven, you love me,
You're with me night and day.
I want to love you always
In all I do and say.
I'll try to please you, Father.
Bless me through the day. Amen.

Night Prayer

God, our Father, I come to say
Thank you for your love today.
Thank you for my family,
And all the friends you give to me.
Guard me in the dark of night,
And in the morning send your light. Amen.

Grace before Meals

Bless us, O God, as we sit together.
Bless the food we eat today.
Bless the hands that made the food.
Bless us, O God. Amen.

Grace after Meals

Thank you, God, for the food we have eaten.
Thank you, God, for all our friends.
Thank you, God, for everything.
Thank you, God. Amen.

Prayer to Guardian Angel

Angel sent by God to guide me,
Be my light and walk beside me;
Be my guardian and protect me;
On the paths of life direct me.

Prayer to Jesus

Christ be with me.
Christ be beside me.
Christ be before me.
Christ be behind me.
Christ at my right hand.
Christ at my left hand.
Christ be with me everywhere I go.
Christ be my friend, for ever and ever. Amen.

Paidir d'Íosa

Críost liom.
Críost romham.
Críost i mo dhiaidh.
Críost ionam.
Críost ar mo dheis.
Críost ar mo chlé.
Críost i mo chuideachta is cuma cá dtéim.
Críost mar chara agam, anois is go buan.
Áiméan.

The Angelus

The angel of the Lord declared unto Mary…
And she conceived by the Holy Spirit.
Hail Mary…

Behold the handmaid of the Lord…
Be it done unto me according to thy word.
Hail Mary…

And the Word was made flesh…
And dwelt among us.
Hail Mary…

Pray for us, O holy Mother of God…
That we may be made worthy of the promises of Christ.
Lord, fill our hearts with your love,
and as you revealed to us by an angel
the coming of your Son as man,
so lead us through his suffering and death
to the glory of his resurrection,
for he lives and reigns with you and the Holy Spirit,
one God, for ever and ever. Amen.

Regina Coeli

Queen of Heaven, rejoice. Alleluia.
For he, whom you were worthy to bear, Alleluia,
Has risen, as he promised. Alleluia.
Pray for us to God. Alleluia.
Rejoice and be glad, O Virgin Mary, Alleluia,
Because the Lord has truly risen. Alleluia.
Let us pray:
O God, who gladdened the world by the resurrection
of your Son, our Lord Jesus Christ; grant, we pray, that
through the Virgin Mary, his mother, we may enter into
the joys of eternal life.
Through the same Christ our Lord. Amen.

Hail Holy Queen

Hail, holy Queen, mother of mercy;
Hail our life, our sweetness, and our hope!
To you we cry, poor banished children of Eve;
To you we send up our sighs, mourning and weeping in this valley of
tears.
Turn then, most gracious advocate,
Your eyes of mercy towards us;
And after this our exile,
Show to us the blessed fruit of your womb, Jesus.
O clement, O loving, O sweet Virgin Mary.
Pray for us, O holy Mother of God,
That we may be made worthy of the promises of Christ.

Prayers to the Holy Spirit

Holy Spirit, I want to do what is right. Help me.
Holy Spirit, I want to live like Jesus. Guide me.
Holy Spirit, I want to pray like Jesus. Teach me. Amen.

Spirit of God in the heavens. Spirit of God in the seas.
Spirit of God in the mountain-tops. Spirit of God in me.
Spirit of God in the sunlight. Spirit of God in the air.
Spirit of God all around me. Spirit of God everywhere.
Holy Spirit, Spirit of God, help me. Amen.

Come Holy Spirit, fill the hearts of your faithful.
Enkindle in us the fire of your love.
Send forth your Spirit, and we shall be created,
And you shall renew the face of the earth.

O God, who has taught the hearts of the faithful
by the light of the Holy Spirit,
Grant us in the same spirit to be truly wise,
And ever to rejoice in his consolation,
Through Jesus Christ, our Lord. Amen.

Prayer to the Trinity

Praise to the Father.
Praise to the Son.
Praise to the Spirit.
The Three in One.

Abundance Prayer

Father, Son and Holy Spirit,
I adore you,
I love you,
I thank you for the wonder of my being
and the miracle of your presence in me.

Prayer Before Playing

Praise God for the fun of it.
Glory to God for the friends in it.
Fair play to God for it.

Prayer After Playing
Thank God for the fun of it.
Thank God for the friends in it.

Act of Faith
O my God, I believe in you
And in all that your holy Church teaches
Because you have said it
And your Word is true.
You are the Christ, the Son of the living God.
You are my Lord and my God.
Lord, I believe; increase my faith.

Act of Hope
O my God,
I put my hope in you
Because I am sure of your promises.
Deliver us, Lord, from every evil
And grant us peace in our day,
As we wait in joyful hope
For the coming of our Saviour, Jesus Christ.

Act of Love
O my God,
I love you with all my heart,
With all my soul, and with all my strength.
Lord, increase our love.
Help us to love one another.

II. The Ten Commandments

Format I

First: I am the Lord your God, you shall not have strange gods before me.

Second: You shall not take the name of the Lord, your God, in vain.

Third: Remember that you keep holy the Sabbath day.

Fourth: Honour your father and your mother.

Fifth: You shall not kill.

Sixth: You shall not commit adultery.

Seventh: You shall not steal.

Eighth: You shall not bear false witness against your neighbour.

Ninth: You shall not covet your neighbour's wife.

Tenth: You shall not covet your neighbour's goods.

Format II

First: Love the Lord your God alone, with all your heart.

Second: Respect the Lord's name.

Third: Keep the Lord's Day holy.

Fourth: Honour your parents.

Fifth: All life is in God's hands; do not destroy life.

Sixth: Be faithful in marriage.

Seventh: Do not steal.

Eighth: Do not speak falsely of others.

Ninth: Do not desire a person who already belongs with another.

Tenth: Do not be greedy for things that already belong to others.

III. MASS RESPONSES AND PRAYERS FOR THE EUCHARIST

Mass Responses

'The Lord be with you.'
'And also with you.'

'A reading from the holy Gospel according to_____.'
'Glory to you, O Lord.'

'This is the Gospel of the Lord.'
'Praise to you, Lord Jesus Christ.'

'Let us proclaim the mystery of faith.'
'Christ has died, Christ is risen, Christ will come again.'

'The Body of Christ.'
'Amen.'

Kyrie

Lord, have mercy.
Lord, have mercy.
Christ, have mercy.
Christ, have mercy.
Lord, have mercy.
Lord, have mercy.

Confiteor

I confess to almighty God,
And to you, my brothers and sisters,
That I have sinned through my own fault,
In my thoughts and in my words,
In what I have done,
And in what I have failed to do;
And I ask blessed Mary, ever virgin,
All the angels and saints,
And you, my brothers and sisters,
To pray for me to the Lord our God. Amen.

Gloria

Glory to God in the highest and peace to his people on earth.
Lord God, heavenly King, almighty God and Father,
we worship you, we give you thanks, we praise you for your glory.
Lord Jesus Christ, only Son of the Father,
Lord God, Lamb of God, you take away the sin of the world:
have mercy on us;
you are seated at the right hand of the Father: receive our prayer.
For you alone are the Holy One, you alone are the Lord,
you alone are the Most High, Jesus Christ,
with the Holy Spirit, in the glory of God the Father. Amen.

Apostles' Creed

I believe in God, the Father almighty, creator of heaven and earth.
I believe in Jesus Christ, his only Son, our Lord.
He was conceived by the power of the Holy Spirit and born of the
Virgin Mary.
He suffered under Pontius Pilate, was crucified, died, and was buried.
He descended to the dead.
On the third day he rose again.
He ascended into heaven, and is seated at the right hand of the Father.
He will come again to judge the living and the dead.
I believe in the Holy Spirit, the holy Catholic Church,
the communion of saints, the forgiveness of sins,
the resurrection of the body, and life everlasting. Amen.

Nicene Creed

We believe in one God, the Father, the Almighty,
maker of heaven and earth, of all that is, seen and unseen.
We believe in one Lord, Jesus Christ,
the only Son of God, eternally begotten of the Father,
God from God, Light from Light, true God from true God,
begotten, not made, of one Being with the Father.
Through him all things were made.
For us and for our salvation he came down from heaven:
by the power of the Holy Spirit
he became incarnate from the Virgin Mary,
and was made man.
For our sake he was crucified under Pontius Pilate;
he suffered death and was buried.

On the third day he rose again in accordance with the Scriptures;
he ascended into heaven and is seated at the right hand of the Father.
He will come again in glory to judge the living and the dead,
and his kingdom will have no end.
We believe in the Holy Spirit, the Lord, the giver of life,
who proceeds from the Father and the Son.
With the Father and the Son he is worshipped and glorified.
He has spoken through the Prophets.
We believe in one holy Catholic and apostolic Church.
We acknowledge one baptism for the forgiveness of sins.
We look for the resurrection of the dead, and the life of the world to
come. Amen.

Sanctus
Holy, holy, holy Lord,
God of power and might.
Heaven and earth are full of your glory.
Hosanna in the highest.
Blessed is he who comes in the name of the Lord.
Hosanna in the highest.

Agnus Dei
Lamb of God, you take away the sins of the world: have mercy on us.
Lamb of God, you take away the sins of the world: have mercy on us.
Lamb of God, you take away the sins of the world: grant us peace.

Prayer before Communion
Lord Jesus, come to me.
Lord Jesus, give me your love.
Lord Jesus, come to me and give me yourself.

Lord Jesus, friend of children, come to me.
Lord Jesus, you are my Lord and my God.
Praise to you, Lord Jesus Christ.

Prayer after Communion
Lord Jesus, I love and adore you.
You're a special friend to me.
Welcome, Lord Jesus, O welcome.
Thank you for coming to me.

Thank you, Lord Jesus, O thank you
For giving yourself to me.
Make me strong to show your love
Wherever I may be.

Be near me, Lord Jesus, I ask you to stay
Close by me forever and love me, I pray.
Bless all of us children in your loving care
And bring us to heaven to live with you there.

I'm ready now, Lord Jesus,
To show how much I care.
I'm ready now to give your love
At home and everywhere. Amen.

IV. Prayers for Sacrament of Reconciliation

Act of Sorrow
O my God, I thank you for loving me.
I am sorry for all my sins, for not loving others and not loving you.
Help me to live like Jesus and not sin again. Amen.

Prayer for Forgiveness
O my God, help me to remember the times when I didn't live as Jesus
asked me to.
Help me to be sorry and to try again. Amen.

Prayer after Forgiveness
O my God, thank you for forgiving me.
Help me to love others.
Help me to live as Jesus asked me to. Amen.

Confiteor
I confess to almighty God,
And to you, my brothers and sisters,
That I have sinned through my own fault,
In my thoughts and in my words,

In what I have done,
And in what I have failed to do;
And I ask blessed Mary, ever virgin,
All the angels and saints,
And you, my brothers and sisters,
To pray for me to the Lord our God. Amen.

✳ ✳ ✳ ✳ ✳

V. RESPONSES DURING THE CELEBRATION OF THE SACRAMENT OF CONFIRMATION

Renewal of Baptismal Promises
I do.

Bishop: N., be sealed with the Gift of the Holy Spirit.
One to be confirmed: Amen.

Bishop: Peace be with you.
Newly confirmed: And also with you.

 Notes

Chapter 1

1   Martin Kennedy, 'Islands Apart – The Religious Experience of Children,' *Furrow* 50, no. 10 (October 1999), 527.
2   *Congregation for the Clergy, General Directory for Catechesis* (Rome: Libreria Editrice Vaticana, 1997), 181.
3   Ibid., 185.
4   Ibid.
5   Irish Episcopal Commission on Catechetics, *Alive-O 7, Teacher's Book* Fifth Class/Primary Seven (Dublin: Veritas, 2003), [10].
6   *Congregation for the Clergy, General Directory for Catechesis* (Rome: Libreria Editrice Vaticana, 1997), 85.
7   Ibid., [12]
8   Ibid., [20]
9   Ibid.
10 Ibid., [25]
11 Ibid., [10].
12 Irish Episcopal Commission on Catechetics, *Alive-O 4, Teacher's Book* Second Class/Primary Four (Dublin: Veritas, 1999), xxxv.
13 Ibid.

14 Ibid., xxxvi.
15 Irish Episcopal Commission on Catechetics, *Alive-O 7, Teacher's Book* – Fifth Class/Primary Seven (Dublin: Veritas, 2003), [29].
16 Ibid.
17 Ibid., [30]
18 Ibid.
19 Ibid., [30]

Chapter 3

1 Joseph Martos, *Doors to the Sacred* (London, SCM Press, 1981), 16.
2 Bernard Cooke, *Sacraments and Sacramentality* (Mystic, Connecticut: Twenty-Third Publications, 1994), 7

Chapter 4

1 *Irish Catholicism Since 1850 – the undoing of a culture* by Louise Fuller (Dublin: Gill & Macmillan), 19.
2 Adapted from *The Saber-Tooth Curriculum* by J. Abner Peddiwell.
3 There are three sources for ideas on the theology of childhood in the writings of Karl Rahner. One of the first places to begin is *Sendung und Gnade, Mission and Grace: Essays in Pastoral Theology* (Munich: Tyrolia Verlag, 1961); translated by Cecily Hastings (New York: Sheed and Ward, 1963). In Chapter 4, 'The Sacrifice of the Mass and an Ascesis for Youth,' Rahner discusses the phases of religious life. In 1977 he published his most famous essay on the subject, 'Ideas for a Theology of Childhood' in *Theological Investigations,* 8, 33-50 (New York: Seabury Press, 1977). The final source is *Praxis des Glaubens: Geistliches Lesebuch The Practice of Faith: A Handbook of Contemporary Spirituality* (Freiburg im Breisgau: Verlag Herder, 1982); edited by Karl Lehmann and Albert Raffelt (New York: Crossroad, 1986). Rahner discusses the faith initiation of children in a section entitled 'Faith and the Stages of Life.'

   For a comprehensive study of Rahner's theology of childhood see Mary Ann Hinsdale, 'Infinite Openness to the Infinite': Karl Rahner's Contribution to Modern

Catholic Thought on the Child', in *The Child in Christian Thought*, ed. Marcia J. Bunge (Grand Rapids, Michigan: William B. Eerdmans Publishing Company, 2001).

4 Rahner, *Ideas for a Theology of Childhood*, 33
5 Rahner, *Mission and Grace*, 224
6 Rahner, *Ideas for a Theology of Childhood*, 36
7 Ibid.
8 Ibid., 37
9 Rowan Williams, *Lost Icons: Reflections on Cultural Bereavement* (Edinburgh: T & T Clark, 2000), 21
10 Ibid., 22,23
11 Richard Louv, *Childhood's Future* (San Diego: Anchor Books, 1990), 5-6
12 'You are so young, so before all beginning, and I want to beg you, as much as I can, dear sir, to be patient toward all that is unsolved in your heart and to try to love the questions themselves like locked rooms and like books that are written in a very foreign tongue. Do not now seek the answers, which cannot be given you because you would not be able to live them. And the point is, to live everything. Live the questions now. Perhaps you will then gradually, without noticing it, live along some distant day into the answer. Perhaps you do carry within yourself the possibility of shaping and forming as a particularly happy and pure way of living: train yourself to it - but take whatever comes with great trust, and if only it comes out of your own will, out of some need of your inmost being, take it upon yourself and hate nothing.'
Rilke, Rainer Maria, *Letters to a Young Poet*, (New York: W.W. Norton and Company Ltd, 1993).
13 Erikson, Erik, *Identity, Youth and Crisis*, (W.W. Norton and Co., New York, 1968).
14 There has been a steady increase in alcohol consumption since the late 1980s. The rate of consumption by those aged fifteen and older has risen from 9.03 litres of pure alcohol per person in 1990 to 12.40 per person on 1996. A national survey carried out in 1993 relating to young people showed that by the age of sixteen, 79 per cent of males and 76 per cent of females had drunk alcohol. It also showed that among children as young as twelve to thirteen years of

age, 8 per cent were regular consumers and 8 per cent were occasional consumers. By the age of sixteen, 41 per cent were regular consumers and 16 per cent were occasional consumers). From www.eurocare.org.

Bibliography

General Texts

Catechism of the Catholic Church. Dublin: Veritas 1994.

Congregation for the Clergy. *General Directory for Catechesis.* Rome: Libreria Editrice Vaticana 1997.

Irish Episcopal Commission on Catechetics. *Alive-O 7 – Religious Education Programme for Fifth Class Class/Primary Seven.* Dublin: Veritas 2003.

Irish Episcopal Commission on Catechetics. *Alive-O 8 – Religious Education Programme for Sixth Class/Primary Four.* Dublin: Veritas 2004.

Specific Texts

Brown, Kathy and Sokol, Frank C. *Issues in the Christian Initiation of Children – Catechesis and Liturgy.* Liturgy Training Publications: Chicago, 1989.

Bunge, Marcia J., ed. *The Child in Christian Thought*. William B. Eerdmans Publishing Company: Grand Rapids, Michigan, 2001.

Cooke, Bernard. *Sacraments and Sacramentality*. Twenty-Third Publications: Mystic Connecticut, 1994.

Deiss, Lucien. *Springtime of the Liturgy*. Liturgical Press: Collegeville, Minnesota, 1979.

Drumm, Michael and Gunning, Tom. *A Sacramental People*, vol. I *Initiation*. Columba Press: Dublin, 1999.

Eliade, Mircea. *The Sacred and the Profane – The Nature of Religion*. Harcourt: Australia, 1968.

Erikson, Eric. *Identity: Youth and Crisis*. New York: W.W. Norton & Co., 1968.

Fitzgerald, Timothy. *Confirmation – A Parish Celebration*. Liturgy Training Publications: Chicago, 1983.

Fink, Peter E. 'Three Languages of Christian Sacraments,' *Worship* 53/6 (November 1978).

Fuller, Louise. *Irish Catholicism Since 1950 – The Undoing of a Culture*. Gill & Macmillan: Dublin 2004.

Humfrey, Peter. *Confirmation – A Community Preparation*. Geoffrey Chapman: London 1984.

Johnson, Maxwell E. *The Rites of Christian Initiation – Their Evolution and Interpretation*. Pueblo/Liturgical Press: Collegeville, Minnesota, 1999.

Kavanagh, Aidan. *Confirmation: Origins and Reform*. Pueblo Press: New York, 1988.

Kennedy, Martin. 'Islands Apart – The Religious Experience of Children.' *Furrow* 50, no. 10

(October 1999): 527-533.

Kubick, Arthur J. (ed). *Confirming the Faith of Adolescents – An Alternative Future for Confirmation.* Paulist Press: New York, 1991.

Louv, Richard. *Childhood's Future.* San Diego: Anchor Books, 1990.

Martos, Joseph. *Doors to the Sacred.* SCM Press: London, 1981.

Mick, Laurence E. *Forming the Assembly to Celebrate the Sacraments.* Liturgical Training Publications: Chicago, 2002.

Osbourne, Kenan B. *The Christian Sacraments of Initiation.* Paulist Press: New York, 1987.

Peddiwell, J. Abner. *The Saber-Tooth Curriculum.* McGraw-Hill: New York 1939.

Postman, Neil. *The Disappearance of Childhood.* New York: Delacorte Press, 1982.

Rahner, Karl. 'Ideas for a Theology of Childhood.' In *Theological Investigations,* 8, 33-50. New York: Seabury Press, 1977.

Serle, Mark (ed). *Alternative Futures for Worship,* vol. II *Baptism and Confirmation.* Liturgical Press: Collegeville, Minnesota, 1987.

Topley, Raymond & Byrne, Gareth (eds). *Nurturing Children's Religious Imagination – The Challenge of Primary Religious Education Today.* Veritas: Dublin 2004.

Turner, Paul. *Confirmation: The Baby in Solomon's Court.* Paulist Press: New York, 1993.

Turner, Paul. *Sources of Confirmation.* Liturgical Press: Collegeville, Minnesota, 1993.

Wilde, James A. *Confirmed as Children, Affirmed as Teens.* Liturgical Training Publications: Chicago, 1990.

Williams, Rowan. *Lost Icons: Reflections on Cultural Bereavement*. Edinburgh: T & T Clark, 2000.

PROMISES TO KEEP